PRESENTING

Lynn Hall

Twayne's United States Authors Series
Young Adult Authors

Patricia J. Campbell, General Editor

TUSAS 659

Lynn Hall and Tazo at Touchwood.

PRESENTING
Lynn Hall

Susan Stan

Twayne Publishers
An Imprint of Simon & Schuster Macmillan
New York

Prentice Hall International
London Mexico City New Delhi Singapore Sydney Toronto

Twayne's United States Authors Series No. 659

Presenting Lynn Hall
Susan Stan

Twayne Publishers
An Imprint of Simon & Schuster Macmillan
1633 Broadway
New York, NY 10019

Library of Congress Cataloging-in-Publication Data

Stan, Susan.
    Presenting Lynn Hall / Susan Stan.
        p.   cm.— (Twayne's United States authors series ; TUSAS 659.
    Young adult authors)
    Includes bibliographical references and index.
    ISBN 0-8057-8218-4 (cloth)
    1. Hall, Lynn.   2. Women authors, American—20th century—
Biography.   3. Young adult fiction, American—History and criticism.
I. Title.   II. Series : Twayne's United States authors series ;
TUSAS 659.   III. Series : Twayne's United States authors series.
Young adult authors.
PS3558.A36987Z87   1996
813'.54—dc20
    [B]   96-12773
                                                                    CIP

The paper used in this publication meets the minimum requirements of American National Standard for Information Services—Permanence of Paper for Printed Library Materials, ANSI Z39.48-1984. ∞™

10 9 8 7 6 5 4 3 2 1

Printed in the United States of America

Photos: Photos on cover and page 4 are by Susan Stan. Other photos and captions have been provided by Lynn Hall.

To the memory of my parents,
Charles S. Stan and Bernice A. Stan

Contents

Preface

As readers, we sometimes take the work of prolific writers for granted. Such was my case when it came to Lynn Hall, who for a long while was writing considerably more books than her publishers could handle. All together, her body of work since 1967 comprises almost 80 books. Of these, 25 are for young adults, with the balance directed at younger readers. Nearly half of her books, including most of those written for young adults, remain in print—testimony to their staying power. Much of their appeal lies in her ability to write convincingly about people and subjects with which readers can readily identify.

Were it not for the horse stories she grew up on, Hall might never have become a writer. Those books gave her an impetus to begin writing and also served as models for her early work. Very often in her books, animals were the main characters, with the humans serving primarily as a backdrop. Today animals are still an important factor in most of her stories, but they now cede top billing to human protagonists.

During my research, I came to see just how much of Hall's own life, past and present, is contained in her books. I was gratified to find her open and cooperative, and I thank her for so graciously answering even the most personal questions. Thanks, too, are due to Kathy Whitcomb-Nelson and Beth Feldman for helping me procure copies of books, some of which were otherwise unavailable; to the staff at the Minneapolis Public Library, always so willing to page the same books for me again and again; and to Patty Campbell for her steadfastness as a series of unexpected events conspired to sabotage our schedule.

"The biographer's worst temptation," wrote Peter Davison, a prominent editor of adult biographies, "is to transform the subject into someone preferable to the original." Much as I have come to admire Lynn Hall—the person and the writer—I have tried to resist that temptation so that readers can come to know her for themselves.

Chronology

1937 Lynn Hall born 9 November in Lombard, Illinois.

1946 Hall family moves to West Des Moines.

1950 Hall family moves to Webster City, where Lynn gets her first horse, named Lady Bay.

1953 Hall family returns to West Des Moines, forcing Lynn to sell Lady Bay.

1954 Graduates from high school in West Des Moines and moves to Denver; takes the first of a series of jobs in Colorado, Texas, Indiana, Kentucky, and Wisconsin.

1960 Marries Dean W. Green; they are divorced after 16 months.

1967 Hall's first book, *The Shy Ones*, is published.

1968 Leaves job to write full time; moves to Clayton, Iowa.

1970 *Too Near the Sun*.

1972 Buys land for Touchwood. *The Siege of Silent Henry*, an English Journal Honor Book; and *Sticks and Stones*, an ALA Best Book for Young Adults.

1973 Builds Touchwood in northeast Iowa.

1976 *Flowers of Anger*.

1980 *The Leaving*, an ALA Best Book for Young Adults.

1. The Solitary

Touchwood, the home of Lynn Hall, sits on a rise overlooking a valley ringed by rolling hills as far as the eye can see. In summer, the view provides endlessly layered shades of green. Those who think of Iowa solely as flat cornfields certainly haven't been to its northeast corner. For Hall, Touchwood is the culmination of her childhood dream: 25 acres in the country where she can live alone, surrounded by animals and answering only to herself. It's the home she designed for herself, and it's where she expects to live out her life.

Lynn Hall's life is rich in its variety, and each element—each part of her life—seems to be planned rather than accidental. She raises and sells Bedlington terriers, and at any given time has as many as eight adult dogs and two litters in her care. Dogs are always around—on the couch, in the kitchen, underfoot. When the phone rings, it could be an editor about a book, a school requesting an appearance, or a relative. As often as not, though, it is someone calling on dog business: a fellow Iowan asking Hall to judge a dog show for 4H or a long-distance caller hoping to buy one of the puppies.

Touchwood (or Touchwood Hall, as the sign proclaims, coincidentally blending her home's name and her own) is a modest gabled two-story house with a Tudor exterior. The front of the house is faced in fieldstones Hall herself gathered from surrounding farmers' fields. Inside the house, the first floor is almost completely open, save for a bathroom and a section along the front that is Hall's writing space. Without inside walls, there is no possibility of feeling constricted. In the center of the room, a round fireplace provides a focal point—and warmth in winter. The second story holds a master bedroom and two guest rooms.

1

Everywhere are photographs and portraits of dogs and horses, some picturing Hall as well.

The dogs have their own accommodations, every bit as nice as their human owner's. Through a door off of the writing area is a small room lined with kennels, homes at various times to adult Bedlingtons and their offspring. Each kennel has a door leading to an outdoor run, enabling dogs and puppies alike to be inside or out. Iowa is snow country, and the runs are partially covered. The first step inside the kennel room invariably produces a nonstop chorus of canine hellos, as does a stroll around the perimeter of the kennel.

On a typical morning, depending on the time of year, Hall might be at her typewriter answering letters from young readers, her back warmed by heat from the fireplace. Or she might be at a different desk—at her word processor within earshot of the kennels, an assortment of dogs at her feet and on the window seat—working on a book, although she writes far fewer books these days than she used to. If it's summer, she could easily be outside with a group of 4H boys and girls who have brought their dogs out to train on the agility course set up near her house.

One of Hall's delights is working with young people and their dogs; teaching 4H dog training classes provides an ongoing opportunity. An organization active mostly in small-town and rural settings, 4H is especially visible at county and state fairs in the summer. The organization's name comes from the initial letters of the words *head, heart, hands,* and *health,* which form the focus of the organization started in 1926 by the U.S. Department of Agriculture. Its purpose then, as now, was to help young people learn skills that would help them become productive citizens.

Some weekends are devoted to judging dog shows; others are spent traveling to sites where Hall can show her own dogs. One reason her puppies command such a high price is that their parents are champions, a designation that is not automatically dispensed but must be earned. Only purebred dogs of breeds recognized by the American Kennel Club (AKC) have a chance at becoming champions.

On weekends during dog show season, Hall packs up her customized van and heads out. The van is equipped with a diverse range of creature comforts. For her, there is the utilitarian (bed, wash basin, and mini-refrigerator) and the recreational (TV, VCR, and bookshelf). For the dogs, there is a grooming table and portable traveling crates—plus, of course, pictures of past champions for inspiration.

Hall shows her Bedlington terriers in conformation competition, where each entrant is judged on how well it conforms to the breed's written standard of perfection. Classes are divided by the age and gender of the animals and often by other factors, such as country of breeding. Dogs in competition are walked around the ring so that judges can see how they move. Then they are posed to allow the judge to examine each dog more closely. Winners in these classes go on to compete at a higher level, where a win can earn anywhere from 1 to 5 points. Winners at each level continue in competition at higher and higher levels, with the top dogs eventually meeting in a final contest for best in show. To earn the title of champion, a dog must accrue 15 points, including at least two wins of 3 points or more. Not every champion will or can be best in show.

A considerable amount of Hall's time and effort has gone into showing her dogs, and she has been rewarded with nearly 20 champions. The increased value this gives her show dogs is only part of the reward; participating in the "show biz" world can be fun in itself, despite the work it entails. Since she first began showing dogs in her early twenties, Hall's enthusiasm for the sport has periodically waxed and waned. On the one hand, the dog show world is addictive. Participants are on the road every weekend, seeing the same people at every show, taking part in a subculture with its own rules, its own language, and its own sense of belonging. Like all subcultures, however, this one has its share of villains—judges who withhold prizes because of old grudges or self-aggrandizement, and handlers who pursue unethical practices without getting caught. Running up against such people and situations can be demoralizing, and, from time to time, Hall has taken a one- or two-year break from all this.

Throughout her life, Hall has divided her attention between dogs and horses. Before coming to Touchwood, she was rarely in a

Lynn in 1992, demonstrating the agility course set up at Touchwood.

situation where she could have a horse of her own, aside from a
brief spell as a teenager. As soon as she could, therefore, she built
a barn and began her search for the perfect horse. To date, several
horses have lived in that barn, but for one reason or another,
none has stayed. The barn's most recent and longest-staying occu-
pant was Tazo, short for Pistoletazo Sin Par, a Paso Fino that
Hall wrote about in *Tazo and Me* (1985).[1] Tazo's talent lay in his

ability to open gates, and Hall would frequently receive calls from the neighbors: "Guess who's in our front yard?" No matter what steps she took to ensure that Tazo would stay in his own pasture, the horse always outwitted Hall. Even the electric fence that was installed failed to keep him at home. Eventually, like his predecessors, Tazo had to be sold. While today Tazo is busy outwitting different owners in Minnesota, Hall has become understandably cautious about acquiring another horse. For now, the barn houses her riding lawn mower and the scraps of lumber left over from building her agility course.

Caring for a 25-acre spread and its buildings can be a demanding job for one person, especially someone with as many different pursuits as Hall. The grounds are far from manicured—a formal style wouldn't be in keeping with Hall's personality at all—but they do require frequent mowing. In the summer, beds of cheerful annuals greet visitors as they drive up the gravel road leading to Hall's house. Down the slope from the front of the house is a swimming pool, a blessing on hot summer days. Along with everything else, there are fences to paint, neighbors to chat with, dogs to train, and kennels to clean out.

Fortunately, Lynn Hall is up to all this and more. While these many responsibilities might seem overwhelming to someone else, she appears to thrive on a balance of physical and mental activity. Such energy contrasts with her physical appearance, which isn't really conveyed by photos. Meeting Lynn Hall in person, one is unprepared for her small stature; she is not simply short but also small-boned. Although she's no longer a trim 98 pounds, it's easy to see the human dynamo that age has merely softened around the edges. This is the woman who during her twenties and thirties worked single-mindedly to fashion a life for herself.

"Sometimes I think about those childish dreams of mine," she has written, "and I realize that there would probably be more truly happy people in the world if more attention were paid to childhood dreams. They probably hold the keys to our real needs. For me, those needs were country and solitude, hills and woods, and a family of horses and dogs; work that was a continual joy and a continual challenge; a sense of belonging to myself."[2]

2. School Years

Nothing in Lynn Hall's childhood pointed to a writing career, and yet perhaps everything pointed to it. She was a child who spent her time alone or with a friend or two at most, uncomfortable with a large crowd. In school, she performed well but was unenthusiastic about her studies. She had little interest in clothes, cosmetics, or popular music, preferring instead horses, dogs, and the songs of Gene Autry. She loved to read, and her vivid imagination—most of the time pretending she was someone else somewhere else—carried her through a lonely childhood and adolescence.

Lynn Hall was born on 9 November 1937, in Lombard, Illinois, an outlying suburb of Chicago. She was the second of three girls born to Alice and Ray Hall, who had each come to Chicago from rural Iowa and were fortunate enough to find each other in the big city. When they met, they found they hailed not only from the same state but from the same county. As a child growing up in the suburbs, Lynn could never get over the fact that her father had lived on a farm and her mother had lived in the country and had actually owned a horse—something young Lynn could only dream about. It hardly seemed fair.

Where Lynn's fascination with horses, dogs, and other animals came from no one knew. Hall reflects that her "clearest childhood memories center around animals" (*SAAS*, 182). Her home in Lombard was not far from a pony-ride concession, and the only spanking she can recall receiving was a result of visiting that place without asking her parents.

When Lynn was 9, the Halls moved to West Des Moines, a suburb of Des Moines, Iowa. Her father, who had been an accountant for Standard Oil in Chicago, changed jobs within the company to

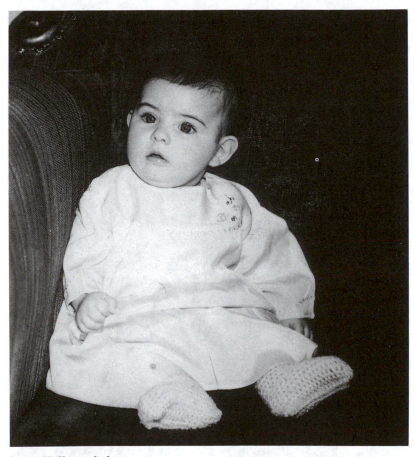

Lynn Hall as a baby.

return to Iowa. This move brought Lynn's parents closer to their families, but Lynn was only marginally closer to her dream horse. She still lived in a town, although 3 miles away was a riding stable that she could get to on her bicycle. She hung around there as often as possible, making herself useful mucking out stalls and watering the horses in exchange for a few minutes' riding here and there.

Meanwhile, Lynn had discovered the library and its books about horses and dogs. Lynn recalls the librarian scolding her

Lynn as a toddler.

Lynn (right) with her big sister, Jan.

Lynn as a schoolgirl.

Lynn on her ninth birthday, November 9, 1946.

"for reading the same books over and over, rather than broadening my mind by reading about children in faraway lands. I didn't give a hoot about children in faraway lands, unless they had horses" (*SAAS*, 184). She read books by Dorothy Lyons and Betty Cavanna, Albert Payson Terhune and Marguerite Henry—any story with a dog or a horse in it.

Dogs—all of them mixed breeds of one sort or another—came and went in the Hall household. Clearly, Lynn's parents were not fond of dogs and tolerated them only occasionally for her sake. Lynn seemed to attract stray dogs, but those that she did gain permission to keep didn't stay long. Some dogs exhibited behavior that caused the older Halls to order them out, while others ran away or were hit by cars. In those days preceding leash laws, being run over was a typical fate for dogs that lived in towns.

The one dog Lynn acquired as a puppy met both these ends. Jackie, short for Jack-in-the-Pulpit, was named after a flower, in keeping with his mother's name, Daisy. Daisy belonged to the Halls' neighbor, and Lynn had watched Jackie being born. She had secured a promise from her parents that she could have one of the puppies, but as Jackie grew older, he developed a bad habit of chasing vehicles. One day, he chased a young neighborhood girl and frightened her, causing her to fall off her bike. The next day, Lynn's mother took her shopping downtown, and by the time they came home, Jackie was gone.

In collusion with her mother, Lynn's father had found Jackie a new home on a farm. For Lynn, this act had even greater significance than the separation from her dog: "the act left no doubt in my logical 12-year-old mind that my very real needs meant less to my parents than their fear of annoying the neighbors."[1] Sadly, Lynn learned shortly thereafter that Jackie had been killed the very night her father had taken him to the farm; he had tried to run back home and was hit by a car.

In 1950, when Lynn was 13, the Halls moved to an even smaller Iowa town, Webster City, where Ray Hall had bought a hardware store. Here Lynn struck pay dirt. She met several children in town who owned horses and kept them in pastures on the outskirts of town. Her dream had suddenly moved from the realm of sheer fantasy into possibility. Her parents, plagued for years by her pleas for a horse, finally relented: They agreed to let her have a horse, provided that she earn the money to buy and maintain it.

Lynn was 14 when she bought Lady Bay, whom she has described as a plain little brown mare, for $100. As she put it, she "became one of the horsey set in Webster City" (*SAAS*, 185). Unfortunately, she and Lady Bay had only a short time together. Her father's store didn't work out as well as expected, and the family decided to return to West Des Moines. Lynn had to leave Lady Bay behind.

Without the solace of her horse, it became even more obvious to Lynn that she did not fit comfortably in any of the social strata in high school. Her experience was much like that of her character Jo Hearne, in *Where Have All the Tigers Gone?* (1989). "You remember how it was in school," Jo says to her friend Theo:

> There were all those layers! There was the top layer, the ones who were class presidents and glory athletes and committee chairmen. And then there was the next level down, the ones who hung out with the top-level kids and actually did most of the work on the committees and were going steady by tenth grade and never had to worry about anything. And then there were all the other subgroups. The one I was in—oh, maybe six or seven of us—was the girls who got reasonably good grades but never had dates.[2]

Time and again Hall draws on this experience of being average—in the middle—while growing up. In her family, she was wedged between a popular older sister who had been a homecoming queen and a cute younger sister who was "already attracting the neighbor boys" (*SAAS*, 186). At school, she was an outsider among the various cliques held together by interests or social standing. Of course Lynn, too, had interests, but they were not the same ones valued by other teenagers at the time. And so she was relegated to a group of girls whose link to each other was simply that none of them belonged to another group. Even among these friends, she was separate, a loner, often preferring to stay home and read rather than join an activity. All through her school years she considered herself average, which in social terms translated into being invisible.

Boys were never even a casual part of Lynn's social life, and consequently it became hard to participate in what Betsy Byars's character Bingo Brown refers to as "mixed-sex conversations." In several instances Hall has noted that she "feared and worshipped boys, setting them on a superhuman level which made it impossible for me to speak or act normally around them" (*SAAS*, 186). Although she herself didn't work through this fear until after she left high school, she often gives her young characters, likewise tongue-tied, an opportunity to discover that they can talk to boys.

When Lynn was 16, her older sister, by this time married and living in Denver, came home to West Des Moines to visit. Along with her came Pudgie, a purebred black cocker spaniel. Lynn happily took on the job of walking Pudgie, glowing "in the reflected glory of this obviously purebred dog."[3] The experience called up all the stories she had read about champion show dogs and fed her fantasies of raising purebred dogs. "I envisioned an acreage somewhere in the countryside," she wrote in *Careers for Dog Lovers* (1978), "with lots of trees around the yard and lots and lots of dogs around the house, all producing puppies. I daydreamed of families driving out to my kennel on Sunday afternoons to buy fat little beagle and cocker puppies from me, puppies who would bring years of love and pleasure to their new owners. This dream stayed with me through the rest of my high school years" (*Careers*, 11–12).

The reality of high school remained miserable, however, and Lynn began living for the day it would end. College was proclaimed to be just like high school, only better. This assessment, considered a recommendation for most people, had the opposite effect on Lynn. Although her grades and ability certainly pointed to college, Lynn was depressed at the notion of four more painful years of confinement in a situation where she felt like a square peg in a round hole. She was convinced that college, at least right then, would be a mistake. Her parents, though they may have

Lynn in tenth grade.

Lynn at 16, in the bedroom where she did her daydreaming.

wanted her to go to college, did not push. The high school principal tried to push, but Lynn resisted; her mind was made up. She
was going to leave home right after high school graduation and
find a job. She promised herself that if sometime later she felt the
need for a college degree, she would reconsider.

True to her word, Lynn packed her bags the day after graduation and left for Denver. She planned to stay with her sister and

brother-in-law until she got her feet on the ground. During this period, her dreams of working with dogs and being around horses receded into the background, replaced by the more practical task of finding a job.

3. Becoming a Writer

In Denver, Lynn took a job as a telephone operator for Rocky Mountain Bell. She was soon joined by two high school friends, and the three of them moved into an apartment. Her friends forsook employment in favor of spending their days with lonesome young men from a local air force base. That summer, the social lives of all three young women improved dramatically. Lynn found that she could, after all, carry on a conversation with the opposite sex. She gained confidence in herself and in her appearance. Even her hair, which had always refused to obey her, became more cooperative.

At the end of the summer, Lynn's friends had run out of money and decided to return to Des Moines; they cajoled Lynn into returning with them, reasoning that it was unfair for her to stay and enjoy herself without them. All three intended to live with their parents just long enough to save some money. Then they would return to Denver. Somehow their plan got diverted, and the next destination was El Paso, where Lynn and her friend Sharol, whom she'd known since grade school, met a pair of twins. After another sojourn in Des Moines, the two young women decided to follow the twins to Fort Worth, thinking cleverly what fun it would be to marry them. Sharol eventually married her twin, but Lynn changed her mind when she got to know the other brother better. She did stay in Fort Worth, however, working for a Texas jeans manufacturer for two years before once again returning to Iowa.

This time her return was very calculated. She had passed the 20-year-old mark and felt it was time to marry, but to do so in Texas would probably mean spending the rest of her life there.

She missed Iowa, and so she returned there with matrimony on her agenda. Within two years she had achieved it.

Meanwhile, in the years leading up to her marriage she continued to work. Having had several unsatisfying office jobs, she realized that she needed a job where she could be around animals. She methodically contacted every veterinarian in the area until she was hired as a receptionist at a small pet hospital. During her two years there, she "learned to do routine laboratory work, to develop X rays, to look with interest into the opened abdominal cavity of a cancer-ridden dog" (*Careers*, 12). She also learned how to groom and trim dogs. Next door to the pet hospital was a pharmacy, and a side benefit of her work was making the acquaintance of Dean Green, the young pharmacist there.

As much as Lynn loved her job at the pet hospital, she found that after two years she had learned everything she could learn there. In addition, the salary was so low that she had been forced to live with her parents all the while, which prevented her from getting any dogs of her own. Once again, it was time to move on. "By this time," she says, "I was seriously infected with the dog show fever. I left the pet hospital for a better-paying office job, got a small apartment where dogs were allowed, and bought a Bedlington terrier. The next several years were spent in office jobs, showing dogs in a very limited way on weekends and becoming more and more sure that dogs were to be my life. I knew there had to be some way of making the dogs a full-time occupation, but I couldn't find it. My ultimate goal was fuzzy" (*Careers*, 13).

A not-very-good solution to her situation came in the form of marriage to Dean Green in 1960, when she was 22. Although she had set her cap for him early, she was already starting to doubt her decision before the wedding day. But she had broken off engagements before; she felt obligated to see this one through. Secretly, she wondered if there might not be something wrong with her because she wanted to live by herself, and she looked to marriage to cure her once and for all. "With a crushing sadness I put aside my dreams of living alone among the hills and woods, with a family of dogs and horses, and belonging to myself. That wasn't the way women were supposed to live" (*SAAS*, 187). She became Lynn Green and moved to Centerville, in southern Iowa, where her husband's family lived. She was somewhat cheered by her husband's wedding present to her, a new Bedlington terrier. Her previous Bedlington had been killed by a car not long before the wedding.

In Centerville, Lynn worked part time writing commercials for a radio station. The local radio station was small and accessible, and she rose to the occasion when she was asked to host a home-making program on the air. Suddenly, married only a few months, she was "Lynn Green, homemaker of the air." The least challenging part of her life at this time was her husband. Even before the marriage, she had realized that she could think rings around him, and now she found it difficult to always let him win at cards and other games. She found little sympathy from her mother, who revealed that she had been letting Lynn's father win for years. In her mother's mind, that was a fact of life in marriage.

More than once Lynn went back to Des Moines with the intention of leaving Dean, but each time her parents talked her into returning to her husband. Finally, after 16 months of marriage, she left again, but this time she didn't return to Des Moines. She went instead to Kentucky, where she had been offered short-term employment at a show kennel. She recalls the feeling of freedom she had as she drove along the highway; she had paid her dues to society by trying marriage, and now the rest of her life was hers to do with as she pleased.

She worked for a dog handler until the divorce was final and then returned to Iowa and her parents. The following years were filled with various jobs as Hall tried to sort out what was right for her. Each time she tried a job that ultimately proved wrong, her focus narrowed. Her job at the pet hospital, for instance, enabled her to rule out veterinary medicine; the blood and gore were defi-nite detractions, not to mention all the years she'd have to spend in college and vet school. Her experience with professional dog handlers convinced her that, as much as she loved handling dogs, such a career lacked adequate mental stimulation to keep her challenged. Maybe one career alone would not be enough, she reasoned; the answer might lie in a combination of careers that would satisfy her different interests and needs.

By this time, she was renting a small house in Des Moines and hit on the idea of raising chinchillas in her basement. The chinchilla is a small rodent prized for its fur, and chinchilla coats were the height of fashion at that time. Hall's dreams of parlaying her chinchilla herd into a country estate were swiftly curtailed when the market for chinchilla fur dried up. But raising chinchillas stood Hall in good stead, because when she eventually discovered that she wanted to be a writer, she was able to buy herself some free time by selling them and taking a profit.

On the dog show circuit, Hall had noticed that many owners had portraits of their dogs painted when they won their championships, and now she turned her attention to this as a possible livelihood. Ideally, if all worked out, she could have her little house in the country and support herself by painting portraits and raising dogs—a nice combination. As for artistic ability, she knew she had some, and she certainly had practice drawing dogs; she had whiled away many an hour in school clandestinely drawing pictures of dogs and horses. Unfortunately, that wasn't preparation enough. "My paintings were pretty good, but not good enough," Hall noted, "and it took me so long to do one portrait that it would have been impractical to hope to make a living in that way" (*Careers*, 16).

Ironically, when Hall first began to think about writing as a career, it was not in the context of her life with animals. She began writing a romance novel as a way of filling up time at her office job. Writing well turned out to be harder than she thought, however, and she reluctantly gave up on the idea. This experience turned out to be the precursor of a more important, life-changing event.

One day in Des Moines, Hall happened to be out shopping when her eye was caught by a pyramid of books displayed in a bookstore window. The title was a new horse story for young readers written by a local author. Something inside Hall clicked. She entered the store to have a closer look—all her years of reading horse stories had made her, if nothing else, an excellent critic.

As she paged through the book, she was amazed to find that she knew more about horses than the writer. On top of that, the story was not even particularly well written. Surely she could write stories at least as good! Suddenly everything came together, and Lynn Hall knew for certain that in that bookstore she had finally found what she had been looking for everywhere else. It was her moment of truth, and to this day Hall remembers her feelings of excitement and happiness as she left the bookstore.

From that point on, Hall's goal was to write the same kind of stories about animals that she had known and loved as a child, and she wasted no time working toward this goal. Everything that was incompatible was cleared out of her life, including a boyfriend who made inordinate demands on her time. Still employed as a secretary, she filled her evenings and weekends reading and rereading her old favorites by Albert Payson Terhune, Dorothy Lyons, Marguerite Henry, Betty Cavanna, and others, looking for elements that made them work. When she was ready to write, she sold her chinchillas and quit her job so she could sustain her concentration. While another person might have been afraid to take such risks, Hall believed in herself and was determined to succeed.

Her first finished manuscript, *Holly of Silver Hill*, was a dog show story. Predictably, because it was modeled after books that had been written in the 1930s and 1940s, it was old-fashioned. But Hall had no way of knowing this and sent it off to Random House, which promptly returned it, informing her that the publisher did not accept unsolicited manuscripts. Hall recalled that there had been a successful writer of teen novels in West Des Moines while she was growing up in the 1950s (the term *young adult* was yet to be coined). Henry Gregor Felsen had spent time at the local teen hangout doing research while Jan Hall, Lynn's older sister, was in high school. Jan took it in stride when she became the prototype for a character in one of Felsen's books and received an autographed copy from him. Lynn, on the other hand, was so impressed at the time that over a decade later she still remembered the book and the author, and she decided to look him up. Perhaps he could give her some advice.

Felsen saw immediately that the book Lynn had written was fine for its time but that its time had passed. Adolescent readers of the 1960s demanded novels with more character development. So Hall went back to her typewriter with a new story, this one also involving dog shows but concentrating more on the parallel transformations of a timid girl and her timid dog. The book was *The Shy Ones*, and it was sent to several publishers. Janet Loranger, then editor-in-chief at Scribner's, where Hall would eventually find a publishing home, sent a lengthy, personal rejection letter. "THE SHY ONE [sic] has now been read and there is a great deal in it that we like very much. All the scenes that deal with the girl's relationship with the dog, the dog's training, the operating scenes at the vet's, the dog show are effective and have emotional impact. The writing is smooth and this is a publishable novel. From our point of view, it is not a Scribner's novel. The human relationships between girl and parents, girl and boy, etc. seem trivial and shallow when compared with the girl's feeling for her animal. The plot is familiar and predictable, the parallel between shy dog and shy girl too contrived. The result is a slick story rather than the totally realized portrait of a young girl." To take the sting away from her comments, Loranger went on to add, "We do feel that you have talent and will be glad to see more of your work."[1] Putnam's rejection letter was also pleasant, though far less detailed and personal.

Meanwhile, Hall was continuing to work on other books but had been forced back into an office job by her dwindling bank account. She worked for a short time as a secretary to some parole officers and then took a job at a small agricultural company's in-house magazine, where she did a staff writer's job at a secretary's salary. Coming home on her lunch hour one day, she found a letter from Sandy Griefenstein of Follett Publishing Company in Chicago, accepting the manuscript and offering an advance of $400. After calling everyone she knew to share the wonderful news, she promptly went back to the office and had the delicious pleasure of giving notice.

The Shy Ones represented a first for the Follett editor, Sandy Griefenstein, as well as for Lynn Hall. Griefenstein had been

Lynn in 1967, when her first book, *The Shy Ones,* was published.

working in the editorial department for a while but had not been given the responsibility of acquiring or editing her own books. When *The Shy Ones* came along, it clicked with her, and she lobbied heavily on its behalf. Like Hall, Griefenstein had grown up in a small town, and the characters and situations in the book rang true for her. After the contract was signed, she became the book's editor, and a successful editor-author relationship ensued.

Hall credits Griefenstein with making many suggestions that improved *The Shy Ones*. When the manuscript had been set into type, Griefenstein sent Hall a letter to accompany the galleys. Her enthusiasm is infectious: "Here it is—in type—THE SHY ONES! . . . I think it has a clean, modern look that should appeal to teenage readers." After some mention of other manuscripts that Hall has sent her, and that she has not yet read, she concludes warmly: "Have a wonderful time reading your book in type. We're all proud of you."[2]

Published in the fall of 1967 for readers ages 10 to 14, *The Shy Ones* also received a warm welcome from reviewers. *Booklist* zeroed right in on what Hall had worked so hard to accomplish, commenting that "the satisfying story is valuable for its full, consistent characterization of the somewhat introspective heroine, with whom many girls will identify."[3] *Library Journal* called it "a good story with believable characters and much information about the raising and showing of dogs."[4] It was also reviewed by *Kirkus* and *The Bulletin of the Center for Children's Books*. All together, *The Shy Ones* received strong notices for a first book. It was an auspicious beginning for a new writer, and it confirmed Hall's strong feeling that finally she was heading in the right direction.

Because Hall had been writing steadily throughout the process of finding a home for her first book, she was able to offer Follett other manuscripts for publication. Some of these manuscripts had already been submitted to and rejected by other publishers. *The Secret of Stonehouse*, which Follett published in 1968, had been considered seriously by Little, Brown but ultimately was turned down. This book drew on Hall's ancestral background, perhaps not factually but certainly spiritually. One branch of Hall's maternal forebears could be traced back to seventeenth-century Scotland; *The Secret of Stonehouse* has a contemporary setting in which a Scottish girl, Heather Mackenna, is brought to a small midwest town to live after her parents die. As often happens with second books, this one did not garner the same acclaim as Hall's first book, although it received a very favorable review in *Booklist*. More important, however, it was an indication of

Hall's early fascination with the genre of mystery, which she has pursued consistently up to the present. *Stonehouse* also reflects her initial work on the romance novel, and *Booklist* described it as "well-built suspense for romantic girls."[5]

With her third book, *Ride a Wild Dream* (1969), *Publishers Weekly* took notice. *Ride a Wild Dream* is the moving story of Jon, the youngest son of a farmer whose wife has left him to care for three young boys by himself. While Jon's two older brothers resemble their dad and enjoy traditional male teenage pursuits like playing basketball, Jon is different. He looks like his mother and is a solitary child with an obsession about having his own horse. This book marks the first time Hall wrote from a male point of view, and she showed herself equally skilled at portraying young males. This manuscript, too, had been sent to other publishers and was rejected before finding a home at Follett. When Hall submitted this book to Dutton under the title *Sude*, the book ended with Jon's death. By the time Follett published it, the ending had been softened.

Hall's next book marked another departure for her. *Too Near the Sun*, published by Follett in 1970, is historical fiction, based on a group of people who came to the United States from France to form a commune in the latter part of the nineteenth century. Hall tells the story of 17-year-old Armel, who dreams of being a lawyer as his father was until he gave up the ways of the world to follow Étienne Cabet and the commune of Icarus. The commune has no need for lawyers, and, instead, Armel has been assigned the job of caring for the sheep. This book combined excellent writing and historical detail with a provocative subject: the needs of the individual versus the needs of the group. *Too Near the Sun* never received the attention it deserved, but Dell bought paperback rights and released a paperback edition in 1972. This book, like the two that followed it—*Gently Touch the Milkweed* (1970) and *A Horse Called Dragon* (1971)—was a Junior Literary Guild selection. By this point, it was clear that Lynn Hall was not only a writer but a successful writer at that.

With several books already published and contracts for several more in the works, Hall finally felt ready to give up the security of the workaday world once and for all. For four years she had been working as a copywriter at a small ad agency during the day, writing her books on evenings and weekends. Always mindful of her dream home in the country, she'd built up a modest nest egg and was now prepared to take the first step toward realizing her dream. She sold the small house in Des Moines that she had bought during the period she was writing *The Shy Ones*. When she bought it, it had been repossessed by a bank and needed work, and the experience of fixing it up was to come in handy when Hall got her country place.

In January of 1968, Hall packed her car and headed for Clayton, Iowa, a picturesque village of about a hundred people nestled on the banks of the Mississippi River. She had read about Clayton in the *Des Moines Register*, which called it a town run by women. That was true, in a way, since the men of the town all worked in the mines and were gone for long stretches of time. The mayor of Clayton (a woman, of course) was quoted extensively, and so Hall wrote to her to inquire if there were any houses for rent. "One or two" was the reply, which was enough encouragement for Hall. When she arrived, she rented an old brick building owned by someone who had long since moved away but was unready to let go of the place. It was full of bats, but at $10 a month, the price was right. Hall lived there for 10 months, making the place presentable in the process, and then bought an old brick farmhouse in a neighboring town.

She finally had her country house, but it still wasn't quite what she had in mind. By 1972, she was looking for land, having decided that she would build her dream home. After months of excursions into the countryside, she found the land she wanted not far from the small town of Elkader. During the first year after she bought the 25 acres, she spent her time walking on the property and planning how and where to build the house. In 1973, Touchwood was built by a carpenter and his helper to Hall's specifications, with Hall serving as second helper.

All along, Hall had been writing for the 10- to 14-year-old age group, but despite working days and being a homeowner, she was still writing more books than Follett could absorb into its publi-

Lynn Hall's home, Touchwood.

cation schedule. Another small publishing house, Garrard, turned out to be a compatible second outlet for her books. She began writing books for younger children, ages 7 to 11, for Garrard. Hall's publishing relationship with Garrard spanned 10 years, from 1972 to 1982, and produced 13 books, all mysteries and adventure stories for readers in the upper elementary grades. Garrard, a small, privately held company, was in the bookbinding business as well as the publishing business. The death of the owner and founder, Bob Garrard, spelled the eventual demise of the company as it existed then, although a reconfiguration of the company in Dallas still uses the name.

This period of the early 1980s was hard on independent publishers. Many of them had prospered and expanded during the 1960s, when federal funds for schools and libraries were plentiful. As the economy worsened, book budgets were among the first to be cut, and some small publishers found it hard to survive the repeated rounds of budget cuts. Those publishers whose markets already extended beyond schools and libraries into bookstores and other consumer areas had a little more stability, as did children's departments that were part of large publishing houses. Some smaller, independent publishers were bought by larger houses and incorporated into their group, often as an imprint; other smaller or privately held houses just folded, and the rights to the books on their lists often reverted to the authors.

Follett Publishing was one of the publishing houses that closed their doors during that time. Follett was over 100 years old and the first of several divisions that constituted the large and successful Follett Corporation. Soon after, the Follett Library Book Company was formed to distribute books to schools and libraries. Like so many other publishing houses during the 1970s, Follett Publishing failed to earn its keep and was eventually phased out. By the time this happened, early in the 1980s, Hall's original editor had long since left the publishing business and moved to California. Hall was aware of Follett's situation and had already decided to look for another publisher for her books for teens; Garrard was still actively publishing her books for younger readers.

To find a new publisher, Hall contacted Irene Hunt, another midwestern writer, who had become a good friend. Hunt had also gotten her start at Follett, and her book *Up a Road Slowly* won the Newbery Medal in 1967. In the 1970s, Hunt had begun publishing with Scribner's and told Hall that her editor there was "a very nice girl" and would love Hall's work. Convinced, Hall sent her next manuscript, *The Leaving*, to Scribner's, and it was accepted. Thus the publisher who had so graciously turned down Lynn Hall's first book, *The Shy Ones*, published her thirty-first book—and nearly 30 more after that.

4. Independence
and Survival

As someone who yearned for independence throughout her adolescence, Hall naturally explores this theme repeatedly in her writing. Armel, in *Too Near the Sun*, dreams of what it would be like to be away from the stifling, overbearing life of the commune; Roxanne, in *The Leaving*, lives for the day she can leave the farm and her uncommunicative, seemingly uncaring parents. In *Flyaway*, Ariel plots to escape from an overly controlling father. While some of Hall's books end just as freedom is attained, *The Solitary* begins at that point, describing the struggle and elation that go into making one's way in the world.

Too Near the Sun (1970) is set in rural Iowa over 100 years ago, where a communal settlement named Icaria actually did exist. Icaria was the dream of a Frenchman, Étienne Cabet, whose ideas of a perfect society were outlined in his book *Voyage to Icaria*. In 1847, he led a group of 70 French people to Texas to begin a real-world Icaria. They soon moved north to Nauvoo, Illinois, to live in the homes abandoned by the Mormons when they went west to Utah. After Cabet's death, a group of Icarians moved to Iowa to start a new settlement.

The story takes place in 1875, almost 20 years into the life of the Iowa settlement. Seventeen-year-old Armel Dupree spends his spare time reading his father's old law books, now marked "Property of Icaria," and arguing imaginary cases in front of an equally imaginary jury. His job in Icaria, assigned on the basis of the commune's needs, is assistant small-stock chairman, a fancy title for "shepherd." In Icaria, a crimeless society, there is no place for lawyers, and the commune has few dealings with the outside world. Armel is already beginning to question the way of life in Icaria when he pleads for the chance to accompany two older Icarians on their annual spring buying and selling trip to Shenandoah, two days away. The trip acts not to assuage his restlessness but to increase it. He brings home a secret, a package of watermelon seeds that he has been given. Contrary to the teachings of Icaria, he wants to own something himself, and so he plants his seeds in a hidden area. For the first time in his life, he will have something of his own, and he looks forward to surprising his family with the mouthwatering gift of watermelons.

As the summer progresses, Armel begins to understand how his older brother, Valmor, was able to leave Icaria several years ago, even though doing so caused his family such grief. Then one day he catches his mother reading a letter from Valmor, and Armel realizes that if he wants to leave Icaria, he has a contact in the outside world and potentially a place to go. He struggles with the difficulty of his decision but is finally swayed when the commune discovers his watermelon patch and chastises him for hoarding. In October, just seven months after his first foray beyond the boundaries of Icaria, Armel leaves Icaria for his chance at the world.

Within the confines of this short novel, Hall explores the universal issues of freedom and responsibility. Cabet's followers left France because that system of government had produced a society divided into rich and poor, where jealousy, theft, and unhappiness proliferated. Their goal was to live in a society where all shared equally in the work and the rewards, where all received everything necessary to live. Armel recognizes the merit in this system when he goes to Shenandoah and sees the poor conditions in which some people live. Yet he is awed by their right to own things and to give them away if they so choose. Armel's experiment with the watermelon plants feeds this need.

In considering his situation, Armel returns again and again to the idea that his father, a brilliant man, would never have chosen the Icarian way if it were not superior. Yet when he sees how many people live in Shenandoah and considers that it is just one town out of thousands across the country, he wonders how so many other people can be wrong. Hall walks the tightrope between right and wrong, never offering one or the other as an absolute. Instead, she paints for readers the gray areas—the pluses and minuses of both the communal and the democratic ways of life. At the end, Armel chooses to explore the democratic way, but not without his own doubts: "Maybe they're right. Maybe Icaria is the best way," he thinks as the wagon carries him away."[1]

The period of adolescence is one of testing limits and acquiring new freedoms, of considering and perhaps even rejecting the values and lifestyles of parents. While circumstances force some people to grow up fast, most teenagers grow up in the way Armel does, with small steps taken one at a time. He takes a trip to town and is introduced to new ideas and opportunities; he secretly plants a bed of watermelons, deliberately rebelling against the rules; when he leaves home, he does so with the knowledge that home will welcome him back if he has made a mistake.

But Armel is forced to make a transition far bigger than just leaving his family to be on his own. He is going into the world to determine whether Icaria is the best place for him. His father made that decision for him many years ago, and now he wants to make the decision for himself. His father is angry: "Fool! You think you have to go out and conquer the world, don't you? You have to prove something. You're not smart enough to appreciate what you have right here under your nose" (*Sun*, 184). In the Greek myth, Daedalus fashioned wings made of feathers held in place with wax so that both he and his son Icarus could escape their prison. He cautioned his son not to fly too close to the sun for fear the wax would melt, but Icarus, giddy with flight, did not heed his father's warning. Hall's title is ambiguous, perhaps a commentary on the fate of Cabet's dream and perhaps a warning for Armel.

Historical novels purport to tell us about the past, but they also disclose information about the present. While *Too Near the Sun* presents a picture about a little-known group of immigrants to America in the nineteenth century, it also reflects the time in which it was written, the late 1960s. For young people who came of age during this time, this was a period of liberation. Disturbed by the country's military involvement in Vietnam, many young women and men became disillusioned, losing faith in a government that did not always tell its citizens the truth. They rejected the material wealth of their parents and adopted a philosophy of sharing and living off the land. Societal rules regarding gender roles, sexual conduct, language, and behavior were called into question and often were flouted. The establishment was built on capitalism; the counterculture favored a form of communism. Group farms, or communes, were glorified as new and better kinds of societies.

Hall's book captures this feeling of transition, of being on the brink of something, and yet she chooses the opposite situation for her plot and setting. She raises questions in the reader's mind and carefully makes sure that she does not answer them: Does the capability to keep everyone fed and clothed make up for taking away individual choice and initiative? Is everyone really equal in a commune? Such questions—appropriate and thought-provoking in 1970, when the book was published—are equally appropriate in the 1990s as we face a global community. How much responsibility does one group of people have for other, less fortunate citizens of the world? The late 1980s saw communism give way to capitalism in the former countries of the Union of Soviet Socialist Republics, the former East Germany, and other parts of eastern Europe. Suddenly, groups of people who were used to being maintained, however minimally, with food and shelter were being forced to negotiate their way in a capitalistic society, where knowledge, skill, effort, and often happenstance of birth determine if and how well one will live. As in any good book, the questions posed in *Too Near the Sun* can be interpreted in a number of different situations, making the book a meaningful reading experience for teenagers in any era.

The Leaving (1980) is also about a teenager's struggle to take wing and fly, but this time in a contemporary setting. Like Armel, Roxanne lives in rural Iowa, but there is nothing communal about her life there. She, her mother, and her father live in isolation in the house handed down from her mother's family. Her mother and father have a loveless marriage and communicate with each other only when necessary; this lack of love and communication carries over to Roxanne as well. The three talk about the weather, the farm chores, and errands into town, but never about their feelings, their joys, or their sorrows. Roxanne yearns for the kind of family her friends at school have—parents who come to see their daughters play basketball and who show pride in their children's accomplishments. While Roxanne loves life on the farm and takes pleasure in the routine work of feeding the hogs, heaving down bales of hay for the cows, gathering eggs, and carrying out the other chores required by farm life, she knows she cannot continue to exist in this way. She sees her mother, Thora, as a woman drained of all spirit and emotion, and her father, Cletus, as having checked out of family life a long time ago.

Hall's story opens two days before Roxanne is scheduled to move to Des Moines, where she plans to find a job and an apartment. She has stayed on the farm for several months past high school graduation to help with the summer haying and then the fall corn picking. Finally, the time is right, and Thora and Cletus have made no objections to her plans. At dinner the evening before her departure, Cletus announces that he'll be taking her horse to the sale barn the following night. When Roxanne reacts, Cletus replies: "You ain't going to be here. You'll be off in Des Moines living in some apartment. Horse won't do you any good there."[2] Despite her protests that she'll be coming home on weekends "and when I get married and have kids I want to have Buck here for them to ride," he remains fixed in his intent. Roxanne looks to her mother for support but finds her face closed, as usual.

Hall's skill at characterization comes through in the way she has portrayed the same scenes from three different points of view. In alternating chapters, the reader learns the story through Roxanne's eyes, through Thora's eyes, and through Cletus's eyes. This technique serves to fill in the history of each of the parents as well as to emphasize the isolation each member of the family feels from the others. Readers come to understand some of the underlying motivations at work in this dysfunctional family.

Thora thinks back to when she married Cletus Armstrong, who came to her parents' farm as a hired hand. Her three brothers had all gone to war and come back "in the form of telegrams of regret." In fact, World War II had swallowed up most of the young men in the vicinity and there were few eligible bachelors from which a plain young woman could choose. Thora quickly settles for Cletus as a way to provide her aging parents with a son-in-law and heirs. But Cletus remains distant, and the pair never make an emotional bond. When Cletus wants to move to Waterloo to work at the John Deere plant, Thora follows him, leaving her beloved farm to preserve an unsatisfying marriage; her life experience holds no precedent for divorce. In Waterloo, they settle into an existence in which Cletus spends his free time with his work buddies at the local bar (and, implicitly, with the women who frequent the place), while Thora tends their home, a trailer in the HiWay Mobile Home Park. Then Roxanne is born, the last brick in Thora's prison. Thora insists on moving back to the farm when her mother develops cancer and needs care. Soon both parents are dead, and the farm belongs to Thora.

Cletus Armstrong also remembers the past, when as a young man fresh out of the service he first walked up the path to the farm. Although Thora was too big to be his dream wife, he liked the way she looked at him. He sized up the farm situation and immediately saw a place for himself there. But for him, too, things turned out differently from his dreams. Thora's parents, though they might have looked frail, maintained their control over the farm, and in spite of his marriage he still felt like a hired hand. His move to Waterloo was calculated to extricate himself but was foiled when Thora agreed to move with him. When, after 11 years, Thora announces she is going to move back to the farm to help her parents, Cletus is not willing to let go of his status as family man, and so he goes too. He leaves the operation of the farm to Thora and Roxanne, however, and takes a job in town at the horse sale barn so he can continue his separate lifestyle. Through Cletus's story, the reader learns that Roxanne's planned departure is providing a window for Cletus to leave, too. While his code of conduct prevents him from walking out on a daughter, he has no compunction about walking out on a wife. He plans to pocket the money from selling Roxanne's horse and use it to return to Waterloo and the John Deere factory.

In preparing for this book, Hall made extensive notes. She provided detailed sketches of the characters as she imagined them and the plot she had in mind. She began with a triad of characters and a setting—a farm in winter. She sets forth a theme: "They don't understand each other because they're so busy talking, no one *listens* to anyone else. Therefore they misunderstand. All are asking for love, yet none is offering it. A crisis time for all three, ending with the father who leaves home."[3] To visualize the plot, Hall sets out a page called "The Rope Pullers"; she sees the mother-daughter relationship in these terms: "pulling against each other but so perfectly matched that there is never any gain on either side. In the end they come together out of mutual respect and need. Father is a catalyst." She writes one story line, only to cross it out. Another page contains another story line, not much different but more specific. Again and again she writes about these people and the basic goals of her book. Eventually she writes an outline of the book consisting of short paragraphs describing the actions and point of view of each chapter. Through this extensive preparation and refinement of her ideas, Hall comes to know her characters and their situations more and more intimately.

The Leaving marked a turn in Lynn Hall's career. After 14 years of sending her manuscripts to New York publishers, she had finally produced a manuscript deemed worthy of publication by Scribner's. It was Hall's thirty-first book, but the first to be published in New York. Widely reviewed and selected as an ALA Best Book for Young Adults for 1980, *The Leaving* received a star from *Booklist*, whose reviewer noted that "Hall has written a spare, tightly constructed story that comes together as a very moving three-character study, which becomes even more poignant with the reader's realization that these three people have lived together physically while being miles apart mentally and emotionally for so many years."[4] It also received the Boston Globe–Horn Book Award for fiction in 1981 and made the list of the New York Public Library's Books for the Teen Age, 1981–1982.

With *The Solitary* (1986), Hall probed in depth the inner resources that can propel a young person to escape a dysfunctional family situation and create a new life of fierce independence. For 12 years, Jane Cahill has lived with her aunt and uncle, having been deposited at their house at the age of five by her mother. Jane faintly remembers how her mother woke her hurriedly on that night and told her to get dressed; she also remembers the sound of a gunshot and the image of her father lying on the bed, a stain of red spreading outward from a spot on his chest—the father who had thrown her across the room earlier in the evening for leaving a jack where he could step on it.

Since this time, Jane has had no contact with her mother, who is serving a 20-year sentence in the reformatory. Jane's life with the Cahills has been an ongoing punishment for her mother's action. She is shunned at school and at home. Her uncle shares his brother's temperament and takes out his bitterness on Jane, never missing an opportunity to denigrate her or her mother and locking her in a closet for three days when she attempts to tell him about her father's abusive nature. And just as her mother could not stand up to her father, her Aunt Marlyce cannot stand up to Doyle, so Jane endures such treatment as Christmases without gifts: "She's not ours," Doyle says by way of explanation.

The moment she receives her high school diploma, Jane puts into effect the plan she has been working on for two years. Her loneliness has resulted in endless hours spent in the library—at first escaping into books, then gaining practical information about raising rabbits, gardening, and the other survival skills she will need when she moves back into the remotely situated house in the woods that she and her mother had abandoned 12 years before. The money she has earned from part-time jobs—everything from mowing lawns and baby-sitting to delivering parts for an auto-supplies shop—has gone in part to Doyle and Marlyce for her room and board and in part into her dream fund. When she bids goodbye to Marlyce and to Doyle (who announces that she's "as crazy as her mother"), she is by no means certain she can succeed, but very sure that anything will be better than living with them.

Jane finds the old house still standing, although in disrepair. Inside, things are just as they were the night of the shooting, right down to the bloodstains on the bed. She fights the memories as she cleans the living space to create a home for herself. Little by little, neighbors befriend her, giving her rides into town until she can get the old Jeep running again. She buys some breeding rabbits and cleans out her father's old rabbit cages. She bathes in the nearby creek on her 40-acre spread and carries water from the spring for cooking and watering the garden. She arranges with a local plant to buy her rabbit meat and finds a pet shop interested in selling bunnies. Although the work is hard, her growing contentment in becoming self-sufficient outweighs her lack of luxuries.

Living and working alone, though, give Jane ample opportunity to think about the past, and she feels the need to understand those years more fully. One evening she writes a letter to her mother, and a month later she receives a response; soon after, Jane pays her mother a visit at the reformatory and learns the answers to some of the questions that have always bothered her. She learns that both her uncle and her father were mistreated as children and that they took this abuse out on the women in their lives. She also learns that her mother saw her act of murder as the only way to save her daughter.

If any one of Lynn Hall's books can be called her signature book, *The Solitary* is it. Although the scenario Hall has created for Jane is completely different from the situation she herself grew up in, Jane's dogged determination and down-to-the-detail planning mirror Hall's own. Hall writes of Jane's figuring, "Thirty breeding does, five litters a year if I push them, six salable babies per litter, not counting the ones I keep for replacement breeders, that makes nine hundred rabbits to sell, at two dollars a rabbit, total yearly income of $1,800. After property taxes, a little over a hundred a month to live on. Not enough."[5] Such practicalities echo Hall's own projections of how much profit she could make on her chinchillas—or, later, on manuscripts—to buy herself the time and space to live in the country.

Yet no violence marred Hall's own middle-class home life in Iowa as Jane's upbringing in Arkansas is marred, and Hall took several years longer to identify her goals. Although Hall bought the myth that females were supposed to find husbands and expended great effort trying to live out that myth, she allows her character to let go of those ideas early on. In fact, when Jane Cahill sets out to build her own life, what she finds is her own identity. With that comes self-respect. At the book's end, the reader understands that Jane may or may not marry, but if she does, it will be for the right reasons.

Like *The Leaving*, *The Solitary* was named an ALA Best Book for Young Adults. *Booklist*'s reviewer, Stephanie Zvirin, noted that "Hall writes vividly of Jane's struggle to overcome not only myriad practical matters of daily survival, but also the negative image she has of herself. The result is an incisive, perceptive portrait of a young woman searching for self-worth."[6] The book received a star in *School Library Journal*, where the reviewer Judy M. Butler remarked: "Bold, sensitive characterization and vivid descriptions of places and events help readers to identify and to empathize with Jane's impatient need for independence and solitude, a need that does not rule out the desire for companionship and for friends."[7]

Flyaway (1987) explores yet another dimension of control within family life and is in superficial ways closer to Hall's own experience. Seventeen-year-old Ariel Brecht and her younger sister, Robin, live in a model family with a father who is looked up to as a pillar of society and a mother who plays her role as perfect housewife. Such a life offers Ariel little chance to be who she is; she constantly must be what is expected of her. Her father's rigid rules control every aspect of her life and her sister's, from their appearance to their behavior to how they can spend their free time. Frank Brecht's family constitutes his greatest possession, and he takes every opportunity to show them off within their small Wisconsin community of Heron Lake. Both girls dream of the day they can escape.

Again Hall portrays a wife who is no match for her husband's willful ways. Mrs. Brecht kowtows to her husband without complaint; he controls the purse strings and doles out grocery money, even driving her to the store and back rather than letting her drive the car by herself. Dinners are regimented events in which Ariel's mother runs to and from the table serving her family, grabbing bites in the kitchen in between passing food and cleaning up plates. Mr. Brecht presides, forcing the girls to drink their milk and eat as he commands. Hall never graces Mrs. Brecht with a first name, reinforcing the notion that she has become an extension of her husband. One time when Ariel complains about her father to her mother, Mrs. Brecht looks at her with "expressionless eyes" and responds, "You must never say things like that. He is your father. He loves you girls, and everything he does is to protect you."[8] In a conversation with a friend, Ariel wonders what could have possessed her mother to marry her father, and although they come up with no good answers, they both agree that at 17 (their age and her mother's age when she married), it's hard to tell how life with someone will turn out.

Hall builds the character of Frank Brecht in a number of ways throughout the story: through Ariel's descriptions as narrator, though conversations between the sisters, and through his actions. The one outsider Ariel can confide in is her friend Marlee, who works for Frank Brecht at the drugstore, where he is a pharmacist (like the man who was briefly Hall's husband, perhaps not coincidentally). Because Marlee knows him, she is not as quick to dismiss Ariel's complaints as someone else might be, someone who saw only the image Frank Brecht so painstakingly conveys in public: "It's hard to believe, in this day and age. If I didn't know him a little bit myself, and if I didn't know what an honest person you are, I'd laugh off the whole idea. I mean, come on, no parent holds on like that anymore. This isn't Victorian times. The whole thing is bizarre" (*Flyaway*, 19). Marlee is a good friend, and she encourages Ariel not to let him damage her. "Hold on to your own strength until you can get away from him."

Like their mother, neither of the girls can have her own money: this strips them of any vestige of freedom. Ariel's Christmas present from her father is a cherished pair of cross-country skis to replace her outgrown ones. One day at the local ski hut she runs across her sixth-grade teacher, who has brought her young son out to ski for the first time. When they inquire about lessons, Ariel volunteers to teach him and receives a total of $60 throughout the next few weeks. She must hide the money from her parents, of course, since she is treading on forbidden ground. But an unfortunate meeting between her teacher and her mother reveals her deed, and her father is livid when he finds out. He storms into her bedroom at night, having just learned the news from her mother. "'You little liar,' he screamed. 'Hiding money from me. Where is it? Where did you hide it? You're not getting away with this, you little sneak. I don't raise lying, sneaking daughters. I want that money and I want it right now.'" Hall describes Frank Brecht's appearance from Ariel's point of view: "Like an enraged dog, he seemed to swell in size. I huddled in my bed, staring at his reddened face. Without his glasses, he seemed alien and oddly off balance, blurred as the world looked blurred to him. At his temple an artery swelled and throbbed" (*Flyaway*, 60). Her father tears her room apart, hurling clothes out of her drawers and snatching off the bedding in an attempt to find the money. When Ariel tries to defend herself by saying she did nothing wrong, he bellows, "Nothing wrong? You hire yourself out as some kind of ski instructor when you hardly know how to ski yourself. You have the gall to charge for your services like some prostitute" (*Flyaway*, 61). His words unwittingly reflect his attitude toward women who aren't kept under the careful watch of a man. Predictably, he confiscates the money, taking with it Ariel's emerging hope for escape.

As spring and graduation approach, however, a new plan begins to form for Ariel. She recognizes that she has something of value to sell, her Christmas skis, and on Senior Skip Day Marlee borrows her mother's car to take Ariel to Madison. There Ariel sells the skis for $150, putting most of it toward rent at a boarding house. On their way out of Madison, she spies a sign for a new architectural firm and asks them if they'll be needing a receptionist—"I've had three years of typing and office computers and business," she says convincingly. When they return home to Heron Lake, Ariel is triumphant, knowing she has a job and a place to live awaiting her after graduation. On graduation day, she feels the shift of power as her father realizes he has lost his means of control.

Into Ariel's story of waging battle against her father Hall weaves a quasi-romantic subplot between Ariel and Jens, a local high school graduate. She meets him at the ski hut, and although she finds him somewhat unattractive, she doesn't feel in a position to be choosy. She has never dated, and earlier in the year, thinking ahead to the senior prom, she had broached this subject with her father. If a young man were suitable and were willing to respect her curfew, he had said, she would be allowed to go out. When she explains this to Jens, he visits her father at the drugstore to ask permission to take Ariel out, and they begin dating. As the relationship escalates, this story line provides a nice counterpoint to the main plot. Jens becomes serious and begins talking about marriage. He shows Ariel off in front of his friends, and soon the same feeling that she has toward her father—of being an accouterment or a possession—begins to take hold in her. The reader can see what her life might be like if she were to accede to Jens's demands and marry him—she would trade one life in bondage for another and end up in much the same situation as her mother.

Hall yokes Ariel's intense hatred of her father with a longing for his love. When he gives her the skis—her passport to temporary freedom out on the trails—she entertains the thought that it might actually be out of love rather than a public display of how well he can provide for his daughters. When she receives Jens's advances, she recognizes how much she yearns for physical affection. All emotions are complicated, and Hall at no time tries to simplify them. This respect for teenagers' feelings is a hallmark of Hall's work and a key to the popularity of her books. Mary Ojibway, who reviewed *Flyaway* for *VOYA*, noted that "well delineated characters—especially the father and the two girls—a midwest setting, and a plausible story make this another success for Hall."[9] *Publishers Weekly* was mixed in its praise for the book, responding to *Flyaway* as "a powerful, unusual story of the strength and determination that can arise from adversity" but also feeling that the story is "kept from being fully affecting by an overly adult tinge to the telling, by a sketchy treatment of a few important elements, . . . and, most of all, by a resolution in which everything falls too easily into place."[10]

The overly adult tinge may be a result of Hall's efforts to provide motivation for the father, which she does in part by having Ariel, Robin, and Marlee act as lay psychologists. Ariel, for example, explains her father's behavior in this way: "The sick part is that he doesn't love us. . . . I think he hates us. I think he hates all women, and for some twisted reason he has to keep Mother and Robin and me under his thumb to kind of, I don't know, punish us or something. Punish us for being female, maybe" (*Flyaway*, 19). Direct explanations such as these do become cumbersome and prevent readers from considering possible motivations on their own. Part of the joy of reading fiction comes in knowing a character well enough to understand his or her nature without being told outright. Yet this book also contains many graceful and subtle touches that enhance characterization, such as Ariel's observation, made of the overweight Marlee, "Sometimes I would look at her and realize that her cage was worse than mine" (*Flyaway*, 15). When Ariel describes her father on his rampage, Hall writes, "His voice rose and split into a duet" (*Flyaway*, 61).

In each of these three books, Hall has written a variation of the same theme, giving her main characters similar traits and still managing to portray them as individuals. Roxanne Armstrong is not the same person as Jane Cahill or Ariel Brecht, but each young woman is determined in her own way to escape from her family prison intact. Each also suffers emotional deprivation, yearning for but never receiving affection from her parents (or, in Jane's case, from her aunt and uncle). Armel's situation is different; he feels wanted by his family and the commune but is pulled away by forces that are more intellectual than emotional.

All these stories feature adult women who have been subjugated by the men in their lives. Together, Hall's stories are observations on the dilemma of women in general, how when stripped of economic power they become equally stripped of their identity. These women have given up trying to preserve their personhood and have accepted the personas their husbands have fashioned for them. The one woman who avoided this role did so at terrible cost: Jane Cahill's mother opted to give up her daughter and spend her life in prison when she murdered her husband. Thora, Roxanne's mother in *The Leaving*, reflects on the fact that she is smarter than her husband, a quality that impedes rather than helps her relationship with him. Armel's mother, on the other hand, has conformed to her husband's edicts, but by keeping secret the letters from Armel's brother she demonstrates that she has not given him her soul.

In *Flyaway*, Ariel's sister, Robin, exhibits an alternative response to their father's oppression. During Ariel's senior year, 14-year-old Robin runs away with her best friend's father. Needy for love, she is susceptible to his advances, and her action reinforces the lack of worth she sees reflected in her own father's eyes. Eventually retrieved from Milwaukee, she returns home with a broken spirit. Robin, the reader fears, will become a woman just like her mother.

The adult men—and some of the teenage males as well—do not fare any better in these books. Hall portrays two of the male characters as out-and-out woman haters. One of these is Jane Cahill's uncle, who has spent his life manhandling women in revenge for abuse suffered in his own childhood. The other is, of course, Ariel's father, Frank Brecht, whose contempt for women is sheathed under a thin veneer of overzealous caretaking. He strives to mold his women into models of perfection according to his own nineteenth-century standards. If they step over the lines he has drawn for them, they are no better than prostitutes—his conception of the true nature of women. For him, and for Jane Cahill's uncle and father, the only tolerable women are extensions of their husbands and fathers. Unlike these men, Cletus Armstrong is not a violent man physically, but he is incapable of affection for his family and is portrayed as lacking ambition and intelligence.

With the exception of Armel, who is a thoughtful, sensitive young man, the few male teenagers to appear in these books are at best self-centered and at worst destined to grow into versions of the men already described. Jane Cahill meets a young college man whose summer job is driving the Freez-Fine truck for the plant that buys Jane's rabbits. On their one date, he talks about himself nonstop, showing little interest in what she might have to say. Ariel Brecht's boyfriend, Jens, is reminiscent of a teenage Cletus Armstrong, looking for a life and a wife to sustain it.

It is clear that in repeatedly creating such characters, Hall is drawing on some of her own experiences growing up. While her own situation was never as extreme as those she portrays, it carried the seeds, and her imagination supplied the rest. Her father, though never abusive, was restrained in showing his love. "Daddy was the kind of man who was a product of his environment," Hall has stated without bitterness. "Such men were not raised to show affection. When we first got television, I watched *Father Knows Best* with tears in my eyes. Here was a father who held his daughters on his knee and called them names like 'princess.'" Again and again she returns to this childhood feeling, working it out in her stories. As for her mother, she notes that "if things had been up to Mom, it would have been different. She would not go against anything he decreed." As a result, both of her sisters married young and unwisely just to get out of the house. Hall took the same route she gives to her characters—the geographical cure. Only after she had secured her independence did she return to Iowa.

Although both her parents have since died, Hall was eventually able to relate to them on her own terms. "When we all grew up and they got old, then I could look back and get a perspective," she reflects. "They didn't understand the kind of person I was until I was middle-aged and they were elderly. And so we ended up a close loving family, but it took a lifetime to get there."[11]

5. Family Relationships

The plots of *Too Near the Sun*, *The Leaving*, *The Solitary*, and *Flyaway* all focus on escape from family situations, addressing directly the relationships between parent (or guardian) and child. Yet Hall has explored family relationships in most of her other books, too, sometimes giving these relationships a central role in the plot and other times relegating them to the background, where they often act as subplots. Happily, not all of her parent-child relationships are resolved through separation or escape; in many stories, Hall provides the means for reconciliation, enabling her young protagonists to find both freedom and love within the structure of their families.

The majority of Hall's main characters are teenage girls on the brink of womanhood, girls who lack self-confidence in their physical and social attractiveness. Such fears are a normal part of adolescence, a sort of obstacle course on the path to adulthood. This passage is eased for those who have experienced healthy family relationships and made more difficult for those who have not. In working through the intricacies of her female characters' struggles, Hall often attributes their sense of unworthiness to the lack of love they have received from their fathers. *Flyaway* is a good case in point; in that book, Ariel comes to recognize that despite her father's ostentatious acts of caretaking, he probably doesn't love her. She eventually locates the root of this problem not in her own inadequacies but in her father's, which is a step toward building her own self-esteem.

Denison's Daughter (1983) is another good illustration of father-daughter conflict, but with different underlying motivations and a different outcome. In this book, Sandy is the youngest of three girls in the Denison family, and she too feels unloved by her father. Her two older sisters are already out of the house—one in a women's commune in California, and the other married (at 16) and living in Milwaukee. After years of living with a father who shows no physical affection toward his daughters and who speaks to them only when he has a reprimand or an instruction, Sandy has reasoned that he is simply uninterested in her. In *Flyaway*, Ariel's father exerted total control over his daughters, but John Denison fails to exercise his parental authority even when his daughters might need or want it. While Sandy interprets this behavior as stemming from indifference, readers soon learn that it actually stems from fear: What if he says no, and they disregard him? A dairy farmer, John Denison is clearly unskilled at being a parent and finds solace in "his girls," a herd of Herefords that require daily attention and don't talk back. His wife is a typical Hall character whose life is filled with motherly activity and who stands in solidarity with her husband, perhaps mediating from time to time but rarely reflecting too deeply on the situation around her. Unlike some of Hall's other adult women characters, Sandy's mother is not disappointed with her life; for her, life has turned out much as she expected when she set her cap for young John Denison.

Two events in 16-year-old Sandy's life further this plot. The first comes in the form of advances by 30-year-old Lonnie Armentrout, whom she meets through the Saddle Club. Knowing that he's married with four young children at home—and that he's a known rake—does not outweigh her desire for physical closeness. She experiences conflicting emotions after receiving his kisses, and she entertains his proposition to spend the following Sunday at a motel with him. Meanwhile, however, her sister Sue returns to the farm from Milwaukee with her son, obviously undergoing marriage problems but reluctant to disclose them fully to her family. Sandy's impulse to help her father with the haying—driving the tractor while he milks the cows—results in a farm accident in which her young nephew is seriously injured. This event propels the action: Sandy is convinced that her father will hate her because of the accident, while her father's concern is as much for Sandy's emotional welfare as for his grandson's physical welfare.

Because Hall has given the reader insight into John Denison's thoughts and feelings throughout the story, the denouement, as father and daughter begin to let each other into their lives, seems neither false nor contrived. It is, after all, matters of life and death that often bring true emotions to the surface and force them to be spoken. Sandy's nephew lives; what kind of damage he will sustain is unknown and unimportant to the story Hall is telling. What is important is that father and daughter connect for possibly the first time, and when Lonnie's truck pulls into the farmyard on Sunday morning to pick her up for their tentative rendezvous, Sandy's feelings are no longer marked by conflict. "I don't want to and I'm not going," she tells him firmly.

Denison's Daughter received a starred review in *School Library Journal*, where Catherine Wood called the novel well-written and noted that "readers cannot help but become aware of the complexities of human personalities and family dynamics."[1] Reviewing the novel for *Horn Book*, Dorcas Hand observed that "the book is short, but long on impact and perceptive characterizations; and Sandy goes a long way from child to adult."[2] Denise M. Wilms, who wrote an entry about Lynn Hall for *Twentieth Century Children's Writers*, noted in her *Booklist* review that *Denison's Daughter* was "not as skilled as *The Leaving* but sensitive and involving nevertheless."[3]

At first glance, *Halsey's Pride* (1990) appears to be another story of miscommunication between father and daughter. Thirteen-year-old March Halsey, the only child of divorced parents, has been deposited with her father when her mother goes back to school full time. This time, however, Hall turns her attention to another matter, March's epilepsy. Her father remains an elusive character, gruff and unrealistic in his dream of building a thriving dog kennel business. March's own insecurity derives not from her lack of attention from him but from her struggle to cope with epilepsy. March comes to know her father both through observing him at work and at home and in learning something about his past. Their relationship becomes close and comfortable as they work side by side showing dogs, but never does it move into deeper territory. Aside from the small kindnesses her father shows her after a grand mal seizure, their relationship is unchanging. As March observes, Clint Halsey is out of touch with reality: "Already I was beginning to understand my father a little bit. I understood that he was a bigger man inside his head than he was on the outside."[4] Among other things, he has convinced himself that his show dog Halsey's Pride is top of the line, despite repeatedly failing to place in dog shows and siring progeny that are susceptible to torsion, a condition in which the dog's intestine twists and bursts.

March, on the other hand, is extremely realistic. She takes advantage of being at a new school to begin again, this time not removing herself from all activities to avoid the humiliation of having a seizure in public as she did in her old school. Predictably, she has a grand mal seizure in the midst of dress rehearsal for the school play, but after a day of recovery she returns to school and faces her schoolmates, refusing to give way to their ridicule and instead educating them about epilepsy. In this book the lack of communication between father and daughter includes the family secret of his epileptic brother's suicide, imparted to March by a neighbor and family friend, Kathryn. Ridden by debt and unable to ignore any longer the curse of his champion dog, March's father falls apart and eventually takes off to work elsewhere. March moves in with Kathryn to finish high school, and by the time her father returns home, March is married and running the kennel with her husband.

This story is told as a flashback, opening when March is in adulthood and on the show dog circuit herself. A motor home pulls up, and out of it emerge March, her husband, and an older man, who turns out to be her father. Clint Halsey approaches another couple's collie and tells them about his own former champion, Halsey's Pride. He wanders off, leaving them in confusion, and March begins to tell them the whole story of the dog, which turns out to be every bit as much her own story. At this stage in Clint Halsey's life, the reader senses, he is little more than an eccentric old man with mistaken memories, and yet his daughter is able to love him simply because he is her father. In this book, the father-daughter relationship does not figure in either the plot or the subplot, which involves the growing certainty of torsion in the line of Halsey's Pride. While Clint's penchant for self-delusion is important to the subplot, the father-daughter relationship is part of the setting. March's growth comes from coping with her epilepsy, and she comes to know herself through the relationships she builds with Kathryn and certain friends at school, not with her father. The dog's hereditary condition echoes March's own; this subtle parallel—which Hall offers but not once calls the reader's attention to—is an indication of Hall's mastery. March resonates to the dog's plight; her father cannot accept physical imperfection, either in his dog line or in his family line.

Hall does a more than creditable job of presenting March's epilepsy in straightforward rather than sensationalized terms. Writing in *School Library Journal*, Sylvia V. Meisner commended Hall's handling of March's epileptic seizure, writing that "this is no sugar-coated episode; Hall writes with insight and genuine understanding of teenage behavior."[5] Hanna Pickworth, who reviewed the book for the *ALAN Review*, predicted that "this should be a popular title speaking to personal acceptance and pride in ourselves."[6]

Next to the teenage protagonists themselves, which the writer usually hits right on the mark, fathers are the strongest characters in Hall's books. They are rarely likable (witness Cletus of *The Solitary* and Frank Brecht of *Flyaway*), but they are always clearly delineated. John Denison wins readers' empathy with his white lie to Sandy in the last chapter of *Denison's Daughter*; he tells her that the boy's injuries happened not as a result of the tractor accident but because he, her father, moved the boy rather than waiting for the paramedics.

Mothers often receive short shrift in Lynn Hall's books, fading into the background along with other supporting characters. In *Letting Go* (1987), however, Hall chose to focus on a mother-daughter relationship, one that is happy in many ways but stifling in others. The relationship between a high school sophomore, Casey Crouse; and her mother, Pat, can almost be seen as the converse of Roxanne and Thora in *The Leaving*. Casey and her mother are close, and Casey has no doubt that her mother loves her. But as the youngest in a family of four children, Casey feels suffocated by her mother's love and need. Casey also is the kind of invisible girl that Hall so frequently depicts—neither good-looking nor plain, neither part of the popular crowd nor a social reject.

Like Clint Halsey, Casey's mother breeds dogs, but she is more successful at it. The Crouses live in rural Nebraska, where their home is flanked by dog kennels on one side and by Sox Crouse's van-customizing shop on the other. The relationship between Casey's parents is relaxed and loving; although they show an interest in each other's work, they stick to their own pursuits. It is Casey who has displayed an aptitude for the dog business, and for six years she has enjoyed the special closeness that has come from accompanying Pat Crouse on weekend trips to dog shows. Now that she is 16, though, being away every weekend is starting to take a toll on her social life. While her friends go to games and congregate at Pizza Hut afterward, she is stuck with having to listen to conversations between her mother and other adults. Casey has become a poised young woman in the show ring, but she regrets missed opportunities to develop the easy attitude with boys that she sees her friends acquiring. The easiest solution is to blame her mother.

Very little action occurs in *Letting Go*; as Denise M. Wilms noted in *Booklist*, "it is the parent-child relationship that is center stage."[7] The conflict is all psychological, as is the resolution. Few events are included to illuminate the characters; the entire conflict unfolds through descriptions of the characters' thoughts and through rational dialogues between Pat Crouse and Casey; between Pat and another mother, Jen Carmody; and between Casey and Libby Carmody, Jen's 18-year-old daughter. Not much tension is apparent even in Casey's conversations with her mother; there are no hysterical shouting matches, no tears, no apologies. Although plausible, the difficulties in their relationship are subtle and therefore hard for readers to identify with. The denouement occurs when Casey and her mother are stranded on the freeway returning home from a show and spend part of the night acknowledging their feelings. Pat expresses her obsessive love for Casey and her fear of losing her to anything else: college, a boy—it makes no difference. Casey recognizes that part of her own self-worth comes from her mother's strong love and that she is responsible for letting herself be smothered.

This extensive self-reflection, coupled with little outside action, keeps *Letting Go* from being a successful book for teenagers. The point of view shifts between mother and daughter, and readers never become strongly invested in the plight of either character. Hall's skill at characterization is undisputed, but somehow she has failed to make these characters into people the reader cares fiercely about. Reviewing this book for *VOYA*, Beth Wheeler Dean wrote, "I found myself thinking of Casey and her mother as whiners," although she did add that "it could be helpful for YAs in a similar situation, since the book's emphasis on the mother's feelings would give them a perspective of the other side of the problem."[8] Ultimately, however, readers never feel the oppression Casey feels, and therefore they never feel the resolution when it comes. Of course, the resolution isn't one, really. Casey and her mother remain in the same situation as before. Although they might understand each other somewhat better, their underlying needs and feelings haven't changed.

Why this book doesn't work is puzzling. When she wrote her contribution to *Something About the Author: Autobiography Series*, Hall was in the midst of working on *Letting Go*, and she talked briefly about her hopes for it. "I want the central relationship to be in the context of a family that is basically happy. There are so many books today about divorced families, step-families, and so on. The dog show setting enables me to limit the time frame of my story naturally. The mother and daughter go off for the weekend to a show. Coming home, they get caught in a blizzard on the interstate. For fear of freezing to death if they fall asleep, they stay up all night talking. They say a lot of things they didn't have the nerve to before and their relationship is forced to expand and deepen." That is the plot summary, yet somehow their fear of being stranded isn't palpable, and by the time they have their breakthrough conversation, its substance has become predictable. Inadvertently, Hall also offers what is perhaps a clue to one reason the characters don't resonate strongly with readers: "During the process of writing, I dig down through the layers of feelings and memories I have about my mother. I imagine the feelings I would have toward a daughter if I had one. . . . That's the best part of writing—going deep into those feelings, memories, and fantasies." (*SAAS*, 104).

Nowhere in her writings or conversations has Hall indicated much about the relationship between herself and her mother. On the contrary, she has mentioned her father's aloofness, and her wish that he had shown love toward her and her sisters. Her residue of strong feelings from that relationship has surfaced in several of the books discussed previously, including *Flyaway*, *Denison's Daughter*, and even *The Leaving*. Her mother seems to have been much like the mother in *Denison's Daughter*, a woman who loved her children but without passion, who acceded to the wisdom of her husband in all matters of the household, including offspring. In a way, it is possible that Hall put her greatest effort into simply creating Pat Crouse in this book; had she known the character better, she might have been able to put her in situations that would have served to bring her alive for readers.

A very different situation occurs in *If Winter Comes* (1986), which was published the year before *Letting Go*. In this book, the roles of men and women are given equal billing. Although the story is structured around the protagonists, Meredith and Barry, the adults also own a piece of this story. This is made possible by the crucible in which Hall places the two families: a weekend in which the threat of nuclear war is imminent. What would you do if you thought you might have just 48 hours left to live? Each character in this book responds differently; their responses are consistent with their priorities and the choices they have made to date, and help to define the strengths and weaknesses in family relationships. *Publishers Weekly* called *If Winter Comes* "a quiet, powerful novel" and described it as "a tense, revealing profile of two young adults and their families."[9]

Meredith is a self-confident, nurturing teenager, and she reaches out to her boyfriend, Barry, but also looks to her mother and father for comfort. Her parents are not divorced but live separate lives, he on a cooperative farm and she in an apartment in an outlying Chicago suburb where she has a veterinarian practice. Meredith goes out to visit her father on Saturday, and they return to her mother's apartment together to spend what may be their last hours together as a family, drawing on the closeness that can exist between people who have chosen different lifestyles.

Barry is not so lucky and is less equipped to cope; his family, though still intact, is committed to the upscale lifestyle provided by his father's lucrative law practice. His father's goal is to turn his son into a carbon copy of himself; his mother has coped with her husband's need for control by remaining "zoned out" on tranquilizers. Responding to the crisis by ignoring it, Barry's father rousts him out of bed on Saturday morning to work on his tennis backhand. But Barry wants physical and emotional comfort, which his father cannot, or will not, provide.

"During that very long, all-too-short, weekend," as Rosie Peasley noted in a *VOYA* review, "the two teens interact with their families and each other in a way that is new to them. Relationships, and people, are changed forever."[10] Indeed, Barry's father is the only character in this book who is not transformed by the weekend's events. Barry's moment of truth is brought about by an old woman he meets in downtown Chicago, when, frustrated and lonely, he begins driving randomly. Her example causes him to discover that he does value some things in the world, although they may be different from those valued by his father. He returns home and initiates a conversation with his mother, who is finally able to admit to the reasons behind her anesthetized existence. For Mike and Lee, Meredith's parents, the possibility of losing each other prompts them to talk about their past hurts and perhaps rethink their future. And last of all there is Meredith, in whom change is more subtle: Her feelings for Barry, as well as for her parents, are simply deepened by what she has experienced.

As a novel, *If Winter Comes* combines the ingredients of success—a timely topic of interest to young adults and an array of likable characters. Yet as Hazel Rochman noted in *Booklist*, it "doesn't have the understated drama of Hall's best novels—there is just too much talking, weeping, and hugging."[11] Hall relies on overly long and sometimes didactic conversations to convey character transformations, rather than layering actions to build such connections. Communication in relationships is important, but sometimes the most important connections are made without words—by small gestures or actions people undertake to show their feelings. In a memorable scene, for instance, Barry stands alongside his father on the porch, separated from him simultaneously by a short physical distance and a vast emotional gulf.

Conveniently, Barry and Meredith, like Roxanne in *The Leaving* and Jane in *The Solitary*, are only children. Siblings receive little mention in most of Hall's books. Many of Hall's characters are the youngest in their families, and their older brothers and sisters are out of the picture, having already left home. This is the case in *Denison's Daughter* and *Letting Go*. In a few books, however, a brother or sister does play a crucial role. In *The Soul of the Silver Dog* (1992), an ill sister distracts the parents' attention from the main character, Cory. The sister's death proves too much for Cory's parents to handle together, and they subsequently divorce, leaving Cory more isolated than ever. In *Fair Maiden* (1990), a mentally ill brother has the same effect on Jennifer's family. In *Windsong* (1992), 13-year-old Karen's younger brother's allergies make him the focus of the family. Not only does he seem to get his way all the time, but his allergies prevent Karen from having what she wants most, a dog.

One of Hall's books, *Half the Battle* (1982), focuses entirely on the relationship between two brothers, Loren and Blair Liskey. Blair, 16 months older than Loren, is congenitally blind. Having spent five years at a state school for the blind, he is now mainstreamed in public school and in the same grade as Loren. Blair has learned to cope admirably with his disability, and he receives continual praise for his achievements. Loren's efforts and accomplishments in and out of school go largely unnoticed. The story is told from both points of view, and the tension between the brothers is evident. Hall conveys this friction through dialogue—jibes that fly back and forth between the boys—and through careful description of their body language, such as tight lips and turned-away faces. This story belongs to both boys equally, for in it both come to terms with themselves and each other.

Loren is at once jealous of the constant attention paid to his brother and fed up with always having to look out for him. Equally unhappy with the situation, Blair resents having to depend on his brother for everything. The complaints on both sides range from petty to substantial. Loren longs for the freedom to be his own person; for instance, he doesn't want to double-date with his brother, although he knows it's the only way his brother can date. He is irritated that the book report for English class can be delivered orally by his brother, while his must be typed and is subject to closer scrutiny by the teacher, resulting in an A for Blair and a B-plus for Loren. He's sick of the way everyone always makes allowances for Blair.

The plot of *Half the Battle* revolves around an endurance ride on horseback that both boys have planned to take over the summer. The Sangre Trek, a 100-mile, two-day ride over trails and rough terrain, tests the endurance of both riders and horses. Participants must train for months in advance, conditioning themselves and their horses. Horses are checked at points throughout the ride to be sure their pulse and respiratory rates remain at safe levels, and horses that have not been adequately conditioned often fail and are ejected. Going on the trek is Blair's idea, but he cannot do it without Loren; since Blair cannot see the trail, his horse must follow Loren's. This event epitomizes Loren's problem—despite having the faster horse, he must ride slowly enough for his brother to follow and thus must relinquish any thought of trying to win the race. For his brother, simply finishing the race will be a victory; once again, Loren's accomplishment will be overshadowed.

Loren's jealously is heightened by a feature article in the local paper that describes the boys' upcoming participation in the trek:

"Competing in the Sangre Trek would be a big undertaking for any horseman, but for Blair, who has only three percent vision and is legally blind, this reporter considers it an act of genuine heroism. Blair will be accompanied on the ride by his brother Loren, also a junior."[12] To make matters worse, a reporter from the paper in Albuquerque picks up on the story and decides to cover Blair in the race.

Loren's mixed feelings about the trek—he'd like to do it, but alone—surface early in their training, as he pushes his brother harder and harder, hoping to discourage him from competing. But Blair hangs on doggedly, even through his horse Sundance's leg injury. Rather than quit, he elects to train another of the Liskeys' horses for the race. When Loren recognizes that his first plan won't work, he devises another one: he decides to "lose" Blair during the trek so that he can make time on his own and have a chance to place in the competition.

Blair senses his brother's hostility throughout their training period, but he refuses to succumb. He hears the subtle change in Loren's tone of voice; he notices small differences in behavior, such as how Loren no longer briefs him on the terrain as they ride. Unexpected branches slap him in the face, and steep dropoffs threaten his balance. When he takes a nasty fall, he hides his pain and gets back on his horse, denying his brother satisfaction. When the final act of betrayal finally does come, he is not altogether surprised.

Hall fleshes out both characters so well that readers feel for both boys, not just for Blair. Loren's acts may be despicable, but they are also understandable. In a sense, he is the underdog in this story, always fighting for an equal share of attention in life. Because he is as sensitive to Blair's situation as to his own, his acts carry with them the seeds for self-recrimination. When Loren does put his plan into action, his voice betrays his guilt. Riding on without Blair, Loren contemplates the consequences and rationalizes his behavior. "But what about Blair? What was he going to say to the drags [the official riders who bring up the end of the trek], to Mom and Dad? That was the weak part of

Plan B. There might be hell to pay, Loren thought grimly, but at least I'll have gotten far enough ahead of him that I'll still be in the running for the trophy. Once Blair and the drags get together, he'll just finish out the ride with them. He'll be fine. He doesn't really need me, just any other rider, that's all he needs" (*Half*, 144).

Loren's plan goes awry in a way that is unforeseen by him and by readers. Lost in the forest, Blair dismounts, and his horse seizes the opportunity to dance away. Blair gets down on all fours and searches the ground for hoofprints. When he recognizes those made by Loren's horse, he follows them back to the trail. Walking along the trail, however, he fails to realize that it turns sharply, and he tumbles down a rocky slope. After spending some time recouping from the fall, he is just in the process of scrambling back up to the trail when Loren returns. Blair's sudden appearance spooks Loren's horse, and Loren is thrown down the hill, his horse tumbling down on top of him. Both Loren and Blair are unconscious when the riders return looking for them.

In a conclusion that is perhaps too facile for the circumstances, Blair and Loren have complementary epiphanies during their separation. Blair's comes while he is struggling alone in the forest: "Maybe while he wasn't realizing what the Trek meant to me, I wasn't realizing that it meant something big to him, too" (*Half*, 143). Loren experiences his as he continues the trek solo: "All of the small rotten things he'd done to Blair during the course of their boyhoods began to gather in his mind, to snowball into this one overwhelming and unforgivable act. God, no wonder people like Blair better than me" (*Half*, 145).

When Blair and Loren have been rescued and regain consciousness, Blair transcends his brother's act of treachery by bringing up the subject of next year's trek. "'You'd trust me?' Loren whispered." Blair's forgiveness is dispensed in a short, one-paragraph speech, delivered lightheartedly. Although the *School Library Journal* reviewer Karen Harris praised Hall's handling of the resentment, guilt, and anger that can stem from a sibling's disability, she found the ending implausible: "The conclusion, which follows too hard upon the climax and the reconciliation, signaling a new relationship that overturns a lifetime of anger, is hard to believe."[13] The *VOYA* reviewer revealed a more optimistic reading of the conclusion: "One is left wanting to overhear the next conversation, but realizing that that first hospital talk at the end of the book is indeed half the battle."[14] In reviewing this book for *Booklist*, Stephanie Zvirin observed that "Hall employs her knowledge of horses and riding to expert advantage as she follows Blair and Loren from their preparations to the ride's climactic outcome. Her use of alternating viewpoints allows sharp penetration of both boys' characters, making clear the progression of emotions that leads Loren to his decision to leave Blair behind on the trail. Convincing and ultimately positive."[15] The reviewer for *Publishers Weekly* concurred, writing that "there is suspense, atmosphere, and excitement in the story, more than enough to make up for the rather suspicious reconciliation that results from a near tragedy."[16]

Some authors for young adults choose to write about characters apart from their families, creating situations in which young people find themselves mostly on their own. Such books have great appeal for young people who are beginning to taste independence. S. E. Hinton's *The Outsiders*, *Rumble Fish*, and *That Was Then, This Is Now* are examples in which teenagers are left to raise themselves, with parents either dead, away for long stretches of time, or stripped of their parental skills by alcohol. A more recent example is *The Big Wander*, by Will Hobbs, in which a teenager and his college-age brother set out on a trip from Montana down to the southwest.

Hall has never been one of those authors, however. With the exception of three books in the mystery and suspense genre that are discussed more fully in Chapter 9, all her stories for young adults are firmly couched in family situations. Even *The Solitary*, which opens with Jane Cahill's move into the woods alone, focuses on Jane's efforts to define who she is in light of her family history; the book ends as she is beginning to become reacquainted with her mother, and readers understand that this is a necessary piece of the puzzle of who Jane is. Similarly, Hall presents almost all her major characters with the task of working through family relationships—be they supportive, suffocating, or undermining— to establish their own identities and gain self-esteem. Only then can her characters be ready to tackle the adult world and form healthy relationships of their own choosing.

6. Love and Romance

Hall's books are filled with tentative brushes between the sexes, first attempts at love that are often rooted in negative family dynamics. The level and quality of nurturing that children receive in the home enables them to trust people outside their families; conversely, troubled relations at home can cause young people to form inappropriate relationships. In *Flyaway*, Ariel begins dating Jens to get out from under the heavy hand of her father. In *Denison's Daughter*, the teenage Sandy Denison entertains the attentions of an older married man, Lonnie Armentrout, because she is needy for male attention.

A particularly inappropriate relationship is the subject of *Uphill All the Way* (1984), in which an older teen, Callie Kiffen, who has little in the way of a social life, tries to make a silk purse out of a sow's ear. The "sow's ear" is Truman Johnson, who has just arrived in town to live with his stepmother, who is married to the local veterinarian. Callie has a summer job with the vet, one step on the way to her dream of becoming a farrier, or horseshoer. It's an odd profession for any woman, but it fits Callie, who lives in a small Oklahoma town. She's been a volunteer apprentice to the local farrier and plans to attend a three-month farrier course when she gets out of high school. Her father supports her goal; her mother is indifferent, as she seems to be to all aspects of Callie's life.

In Truman, Callie sees the perfect opportunity to round out her life—never mind that he is lazy and has just come out of a juvenile correctional program. Her determination to change him into boyfriend material extends to finding him a ranch job (at which he stays only two days) and covering for him when she finds out that he has been breaking into vending machines. Ultimately, Truman's crimes come home to Callie—he steals her prize truck to use in a break-in. When the police trace the truck to her, she finally reveals what she knows about him, relinquishing all hope of that silk purse.

Callie must experience firsthand what adults already know, that changing another person is indeed an uphill and fruitless task unless that person wants to change. Her father gently tries to steer her away from Truman, but in his wisdom he does not forbid her to see him. "Callie's warm relationship with her father is one of the best parts of this novel," wrote the reviewers for *English Journal* in an article focusing on the YA problem novel. "Pop can see that Truman is a loser but doesn't stop Callie's salvage attempts." As a result, they note, Callie "learns some valuable lessons about herself and about choices we all have to make."[1]

Hall's penchant for situating stories in the lives of ordinary people living outside the mainstream is at work here, a fact not lost on the *Booklist* reviewer Stephanie Zvirin, who recommended the book for junior high and high school readers. "Hall again works her magic in a rural setting," she observed, "and her artless narrator/protagonist with the down-home style of speech is a gem whose genuineness more than compensates for some leanness of plot."[2]

Many of the romantic involvements in Hall's books are between teenage girls and older men. One book built entirely around such an experience is *The Giver* (1985), a strong book that received almost unanimous praise from reviewers when it was published. Writing in *Horn Book*, Anita Silvey proclaimed that "in *The Giver*, Hall has crafted a teenage romance that transcends the usual parameters of such a novel."[3] *The Giver* is the story of 15-year-old Mary McNeal, daughter of an affable insurance representative, Mackie McNeal, and a respected special education teacher, Rosemary McNeal; and middle sister to Annette and Beth. This family is as normal as they get: They go out for breakfast at Hardee's before church every Sunday; they eat tuna casserole; they play Scrabble at night. The only drawback is that

Mr. McNeal is frequently absent in the evening, out making calls on potential clients. Clues are dropped early on that McNeal, an aging former big-man-on-campus, is prone to extramarital affairs. When this becomes concrete for Mary, her first thought is that, if her capable and giving mother can't keep her father's love, how in the world can someone as "blah" as *she* is expect to be loved?

Mary's homeroom teacher, Mr. Flicket, sees more in her than blahness; he sees a sharp mind and a face beautiful with innocence. He calls her a slow bloomer and tells her that she'll "bloom better and last longer."[4] Mary fixates on Mr. Flicket, a fortyish bachelor who lives with his mother, and she lives for glimpses of him in class and hallway. James Flicket, the reader finds out, does have a special attraction to Mary, an attraction that is born of the loneliness imposed by his demanding mother. When the entire class repairs to Mr. Flicket's barn to work on the homecoming float, Mary meets the dour old lady, who observes the way her son singles Mary out. "You need to be careful of that sort of thing, James," his mother warns him later. "You've been through it before. You ought to be able to recognize the symptoms by now and discourage it at the beginning" (*Giver*, 44–45). This ominous warning sets readers on edge, wondering which way the story will go.

Mr. Flicket has always done as his mother said, and in a conversation with Mary that verges on preachiness, he explains why Mary must forgo her special feelings for him: "It could destroy my life and do serious damage to yours." This book focuses entirely on Mary's crush on her teacher and on his feelings for her and describes her family life only as a backdrop. What happens in the family is of secondary importance to the plot and in no way informs Mary's character. (And what happens is a lot, since her father's girlfriend poses as a color consultant and assuages her curiosity about "the wife" by making a house call on Mrs. McNeal, whereupon Mr. McNeal walks in the door and the ruse comes to light.) Mary's character development is left entirely to Mr. Flicket, on whom Hall puts the onus of the resolution and whose wise words allow Mary to feel confidence in herself despite his rejection. The story belongs to both Mary and her teacher, one entering her prime and the other having passed his.

Hall has displayed a restrained hand in portraying this adolescent crush. The *Booklist* reviewer Hazel Rochman noted that "except for a too-neat ending, she treats with respect and delicacy a teacher-pupil relationship that is too often dismissed with a mocking stereotype."[5] *The Bulletin of the Center for Children's Books* called this book "Lynn Hall at her best, in a story that is poignant and potent, a story of love that is wise and altruistic . . . written with insight and craft."[6]

Although readers expect contemporary settings from Hall, from the opening page of *Fair Maiden* (1990) one might think that Lynn Hall has written a historical romance: "She stood motionless before the walled city, the fog wrapping close around her, then wafting away to leave her exposed in a shaft of early-morning sun."[7] The illusion is quickly shattered as the reader turns the page and encounters the sounds of modern life, a car door slamming and a noisy jet overhead. As it turns out, this is another contemporary story of romance between a teenage girl and an older man, but this romance is consummated.

The "fair maiden" is Jennifer Dean, a high school student dressed for her role at the Renaissance Fair, an annual fall event that offers six weekends of life in a recreated medieval English village. Each weekend morning, Jennifer shuttles between home and fair, shedding her contemporary concerns for a fifteenth-century persona. As Guinevere, she finds herself considerably less inhibited and enjoys responding to the flirtatious remarks that come her way.

Home life isn't all that great for Jennifer; her father and mother have been divorced since she was two, and her brother Michael's violent behavior has landed him in a detention facility, where he is receiving treatment. Michael's erratic behavior, which has included holding both her mother and Jennifer at knifepoint at different times, has driven away the stepfather that Jennifer adored; she blames both men for this loss. Her mother has coped by excelling as a financial planner and throwing herself into the dating scene. At times it is unclear who is the more mature, Jennifer or her mother.

When Jennifer catches the eye of John the Lutanist, a wandering minstrel, the figure of her stepfather pops unbidden into her mind. John, a thirtyish young man, symbolizes strength and caring; best of all, he exists completely apart from everyday reality. By providing its two settings, this short novel sets up a clear distinction between fantasy and reality. On weekends there are no concerns of past or future as all pretend to be something they're not; during the week, Jennifer is back to being a high school student, fighting to keep up her grades and at the same time having to mother her mother. But the line between fantasy and reality is not always so easy to distinguish. As Guinevere spends more time with John the Lutanist, Jennifer thinks she is falling in love with the man; his reluctance to step out of character during their times alone frustrates her. Conversely, on the home front her mother continues the fantasy that Michael is getting better and that theirs will be a happy home life when he is released shortly; her severe headaches belie her pretensions.

Predictably, reality invades both settings. Jennifer's romance with John leads to a carefully planned sexual tryst in his trailer; she should feel glorious, but instead she feels let down. Michael's return to the family ends in a bloody, violent conflict that puts Jennifer's mother in the hospital and leaves Jennifer with bruises and a possible concussion. The reality is that Jennifer has had unprotected sex with a kind man who without the trappings of his medieval character holds little appeal for her. The other reality is that her brother truly is mentally ill.

All this reality, however, is presented in fairly unrealistic terms. The conversations in which Jennifer works out her feelings and thoughts about what's happened in her life read more like exposition than truth. Hall's mistake here may have been to tell too much, to tie up the psychological ends too neatly. In doing so, she underestimates the reader's ability to sort out the conflicting feelings that can occur when a young woman loses her virginity to a man she doesn't love. "It wasn't really him I fell in love with," she rationalizes. "He was just a face, a song. What I fell in love with was my own idea of him, what I needed him to be. Like I was projecting onto a movie screen or something. It was coming out of me, not out of him" (*Maiden*, 114–15). Most young women in this situation don't recognize reasons beyond the immediate; it takes hindsight to accomplish that. But Jennifer seems to have classified her motivations and dispensed with her feelings in a single conversation, which has freed her to be lighthearted at the book's end.

In a roundup of books for the teenage reader, the *English Journal* editors Elizabeth A. Belden and Judith M. Beckman had nothing but praise for *Fair Maiden*. "Quality work sometimes comes in slender volumes," they noted. "Lynn Hall presents a high-school senior's first love experience with a satisfying richness rarely accomplished so quickly."[8] The *Booklist* reviewer Stephanie Zvirin, on the other hand, found the novel's brevity a symptom of deeper flaws. The book received a boxed review, a vehicle garnering it above-average attention. "There's no question teens will read this novel: the romance fairly crackles as it moves toward the inevitable sex, which is handled with great reserve, and Hall does a creditable job of manipulating two different settings. But readers deserve more about characters and relationships—especially about scary yet tantalizing Michael, who's presented as an important factor in Jennifer's life—and the book gets heavy-handed after the sex, with a secondary character ready in the wings to take John's place and offer Jennifer words of wisdom. . . . The makings of a good novel are certainly here: romance, tension, intriguing characters. But in what may have been a desire to keep her books short (most of her novels are), Hall has shortchanged her readers."[9]

Ann W. Moore, who reviewed this book for *School Library Journal*, was also disappointed: "Jennifer's difficult family situation is both underdeveloped and poorly integrated into the text; the subplot of the psychopathic brother is nearly irrelevant. Hall introduces themes with great potential from time to time, but they all fade out."[10]

In another book published the year after *Fair Maiden*, Hall returned to the subject of romance between a teenage girl and an older man. But as the title, *Flying Changes* (1991), indicates, Denny Browner's sexual fling with Tyler Oneota is only one of many changes she is undergoing at the same time. In horse parlance, *flying change* refers to a horse's ability to change direction without breaking its lope. The horse Denny is training is resisting the right flying lead change by either stumbling or bucking each time she attempts it.

The circumstances of Denny's life are requiring that she, too, change direction without stopping or stumbling. Her father, who makes his living as a rodeo cowboy, has sustained a paralyzing injury and will soon be returning home to Kansas from Colorado, where he has been hospitalized after his accident. Her mother, absent for years, has made a sudden and puzzling reappearance in their lives. Gramma B., who has raised Denny, feels put out at her daughter-in-law's return and takes an apartment in town. In the midst of it all, Denny must deal with her feelings for Tyler, her father's roping partner—a muscular, rangy, handsome cowboy younger than her father but considerably older and more worldly than Denny. Her charge is to learn to take these changes in stride, and she does so by dint of hard work and concentration, in much the same way she finally teaches her horse to make the flying change.

Readers can see that Denny's relationship with Tyler is flawed from the start. He's a roamer, on the rodeo circuit much of the time. He's stayed at Gramma and Denny's before, giving Denny ample time to watch his steady stream of girlfriends. But this time Denny is older, and the chemistry has changed; she is particularly susceptible to his charms and deludes herself into thinking that he sees something special in her. Playful pats on the rear give way to more deliberate hugs and culminate in lovemaking (referred to but not described in the text) on the evening before Tyler is set to hit the road again. The next day, Denny waits for his declaration of love and promise of faithfulness; instead, she gets a perfunctory kiss goodbye as he says, "So long, Denny. You be good now."[11]

Although Denny recognizes at once that in Tyler's eyes she's no different from all the others, accepting that fact takes longer.

Over the five-day span of the story, she ponders the meaning and the consequences of her sexual act with Tyler as she copes with everything else: her mother's arrival, her father's return in a wheelchair, her grandmother's departure for town. Unlike Jennifer in *Fair Maiden*, Denny cannot dismiss what has happened lightly, and it serves to deepen her understanding of the people around her. Only at the end of the story, when she is triumphant in having trained the horse to make the flying lead change and has therefore secured its sale for a much-needed $3,500, does she realize that she has gotten through the whole day—almost—without thinking about Tyler. While having sex certainly doesn't make her into an adult, helping shoulder responsibility for the family does.

Flying Changes was given a starred review in *Booklist*. Hazel Rochman called this "Hall at her best" and pointed out that none of the characters is formulaic or stereotypical.[12] Rita, Denny's mother, may look and act like a floozy but has her feet on the ground. She brings her dog grooming equipment with her and sets up shop, and it's she who figures out how to generate income from the lackluster saddle shop alongside the house. Gramma B. is a feisty woman who's not afraid to share with Denny her own life's hopes and disappointments. Doe, Denny's father, has been both a caring father and a womanizer. Tyler is the only flat character, which suits him perfectly; he is what he appears to be on the outside, and nothing more.

Charlene Strickland's perceptive review for *School Library Journal* focused on the theme of the book, "relationships between men and women, and how they shift from love to resentment."[13] She taps into the very heart of the book, which poses the question of what romantic love is. For Rita, Denny's mother, it was falling for a cowboy who didn't curb his woman-chasing ways after marriage. Her solution was to take off, but a decade later, when fate curbs those impulses for him, she's back. For Gramma, love is living with a husband who let go of his rodeo dream too early. Did he do it for her, or was she simply a handy way out of having to find his own measure? She'll never know the answer, but she has paid for his unhappiness in small ways throughout her marriage. As for Denny, she has learned so far only what romantic love is *not:* It's not simply sex.

Rare is the book in which Hall portrays sustained romantic relationships that are based on mutual respect and liking. In *The Solitary*, Jane Cahill has a couple of dates with a college boy she meets in the course of selling her rabbits to the Freez-Fine company. Aaron is pinch-hitting for his father, driving the truck that picks up fryer-sized rabbits from breeders in the region. Good-looking and self-confident, he is exactly the kind of young man that renders Jane incapable of speech, and she comes away from their meeting equally elated by two events: She has made her first sale (for $120, no less) and she has been flirted with. Although he is away at college much of the time, Aaron makes unpredictable appearances in Jane's life, showing up at her cabin unexpectedly one Sunday and on another inviting her to a nearby town for a rabbit show. That date, during which he monopolizes the conversation by talking exclusively about himself, ends back at her cabin with a kiss and Aaron's attempt to steer Jane toward the bed. She refuses, and he responds with equanimity but leaves shortly thereafter, never to be seen again. However brief, this is her first involvement with a member of the opposite sex; it provides her with fodder for dreams but little else. Ironically, the paperback publishers selected one of these scenes to depict on the front cover of *The Solitary*, presumably hoping to entice readers with a promise of romance. In reality, the romance is one-sided, and the promise is false.

In one of their few conversations, Aaron remarked that Jane's problem was that she was too independent. "You give the impression that you don't need anyone for anything." (*Solitary*, 72). While Jane has proved that she does not need to depend on anyone for her physical survival, she does need someone for emotional support. Her ability to take care of herself requires that she be in a relationship of mutual respect and understanding, not one in which she must efface herself by taking the role of adoring girlfriend.

In *The Leaving*, Hall portrays the other extreme that strong young women must contend with—being the object of adoration.

This is Roxanne's experience with Randy, the young man she begins dating after she moves to Des Moines. Randy is described as "a big soft young man who always seemed to be coming untucked or unzipped around the middle" (*Leaving*, 110). He is genuinely nice but unexciting, and Roxanne senses that he is clearly interested in settling down with her. Although his civil service job at the post office offers stability, it also offers a future she finds too predictable: "a little house out in some subdivision, and then babies" (*Leaving*, 110). Although part of Roxanne finds this comforting, in the end she faces the realization that the picture doesn't work with Randy in it; under different circumstances, she might want those things, but she doesn't want Randy. Forgoing the known for the unknown is always a risk, but that's what Roxanne does by returning to live on the farm. Will she find the kind of love she is looking for? Whether or not she does, she will take responsibility for whatever happens in her life. Like all of Hall's main characters who find themselves in similar situations, she remains true to her own nature.

7. Friendship

Friends are paramount in the lives of adolescents. Ask teenagers whom they confide in or talk to when they have a problem, and the answer will inevitably be a friend rather than a parent. Good friends are supportive without being judgmental; they share one another's concerns and outlook. Peer groups offer a sense of belonging, and in some cases they can exert considerably more influence than family. Peer groups also have the power to keep people out, isolating a classmate and earmarking her or him as a permanent outsider.

While many young adult books center on the often rocky process of establishing real friendships and finding one's place in the social web of town or school, few of Lynn Hall's books focus on these themes. Usually, friends play only a minor role in most of Hall's books; by and large they are supporting characters who serve as sounding boards as the protagonists attempt to sort through the complexities of family or romantic relationships. In *Flyaway*, for example, Ariel Brecht's best friend, Marlee, not only listens patiently and compassionately as Ariel recounts stories of how Mr. Brecht treats his family but also risks her job (she works for Mr. Brecht at the drugstore) to help Ariel escape. Part of what makes Marlee such a good friend is that she believes in Ariel implicitly rather than accepting Mr. Brecht's carefully crafted public persona, as other listeners might be tempted to do.

So, too, does Denny Browner head straight for her friend, Sue, when she's feeling bad about Tyler's leaving town in *Flying Changes*. Sue's family—intact, with educated parents and a nice house in town—couldn't be more different from Denny's, and yet their friendship has remained strong since grade school. When in seventh grade their classmates got wind of a story circulating around town about how Denny's father was caught messing around with a married woman, it was Sue who stood up for Denny, reminding the other seventh-graders that "we can't none of us control what our parents do" (*Changes*, 33). Sue knows that the only comfort she can give Denny is to be there; nothing she can say will lessen the heartbreak.

Only occasionally does friendship emerge as the main theme in Hall's work, but when it does, the author adds her own characteristic twist, anticipating by one and even two decades some current trends in subject matter. Such is the case with *The Siege of Silent Henry* (1972), which deals with a friendship between two people of vastly different ages; and *Just One Friend* (1985), which looks at the world from the point of view of someone who has been classified as a slow learner. These two books are fascinating explorations of perceptions of friendship, as is Hall's *Sticks and Stones* (1972), a pivotal book that chronicles the growing friendship between two young men, one of whom is gay.

In 1972, when *The Siege of Silent Henry* was published, *intergenerational* was not the buzzword that it became in the 1990s. In this book, real friendship develops between the town eccentric, Henry Leffert; and a neighbor, Robert Short, who is in high school. Robert is a calculating young man; he has discovered how to please his teachers by deducing a need or weakness and then supplying it—he calls this the RS Theory of Teacher Handling. Now he is applying the theory to old Henry to get him to divulge the location of his ginseng beds, which can yield thousands of dollars' worth of the rare herb each year. Robert, who is already on his way to entrepreneurship by raising chinchillas in the basement, is bound and determined to have $10,000 in the bank by the time he gets out of college, and he views Henry as just another step in this plan.

Henry, lonely as can be, sees through Robert's flattery immediately but soaks it up anyway. Henry has some secrets beyond the location of the ginseng beds, including a wife he walked out on 20 years ago. To protect himself, he's gotten into the habit of saying very little, thus earning the sobriquet "Silent Henry." He likes having Robert to talk with, and Robert, for his part, finds himself enjoying Henry's company and feeling unpleasantly disturbed each time he remembers why he's courting Henry's favor.

Robert's parents are perfect role models for someone whose chief goal is a materialistic lifestyle. His father manages the silica mine, and the family lives in Buck Creek's biggest house, which Robert's mother has decorated with impeccable taste. They encourage the boy's preoccupation with money and even joke about it between themselves, wondering how they managed to raise such a smart son. At no time do moral or ethical considerations complicate their view of the world. One evening at dinner Robert reports how he was chastised for hogging the ball in gym class, putting his own spin on the story, of course. His mother's first impulse is to bring it up at the next school board meeting: "I think that's terrible. . . . Teachers should encourage the superior students instead of trying to hold them down to the level of the poorer ones, even in sports."[1] Garnering attention is evidently more important in this family than good sportsmanship. Even worse, when Robert tells his father that his male chinchilla has passed on the trait of fur-chewing to his progeny, reducing his value from $300 as a stud to a mere $50 as a pelt, his father reminds him of the old axiom *caveat emptor*. The animal looks good, and if the buyer doesn't ask about bad habits, why mention it? "I'd certainly think twice about passing up three hundred dollars, if I were you," he says, leaving Robert strangely disappointed in his father (*Siege*, 128). When Robert describes the same situation to Henry, he gets a different motto: "Honesty is the best policy." Robert experiences uncomfortable feelings about some of his actions and wonders why his parents don't help him distinguish right from wrong.

Despite his advice to Robert, Henry isn't feeling so honest himself. He is thinking about how his life in Buck Creek is really a sham. He's living without permission in the house that his late friend Harold owned; the townspeople assume Harold willed it to him, but Henry has no idea who really owns it, and each day brings the fear that he will be found out. And, of course, there's the matter of the wife he walked out on in another town.

Robert's conversations make Henry more aware of his own loose ends than ever, and this awareness begins to eat at him.

Thus the "friendship," which begins as a game for Robert and a welcome diversion for Henry, profoundly affects the lives of both men. Robert begins to genuinely like Henry and to admire his strength of character and, in turn, is sensitized to how he relates to other people. Henry realizes that Robert perceives him as "a good person"; should the truth come to light, he fears Robert's estimation of him would plunge. This line of thinking results in only one option for Henry, to leave Buck Creek: "I'll go, and the boy won't ever know but what I really was the good kind of person he took me to be" (*Siege*, 135–36). He loads his station wagon and heads out of town, leaving a ginseng root shaped like a little man in Robert's mailbox as a parting gift.

This is an O. Henry ending if there ever was one, full of surprise and irony. Finally, Robert has found an adult he cannot manipulate and sees Henry as someone to turn to for moral guidance. Conversely, for the first time Henry learns what it feels like to be viewed with respect rather than as an oddity. But to preserve that respect, Henry must leave. Paradoxically, the one genuine friendship Robert has ever had is based on lies and deception.

At the same time that Henry is packing his belongings in the wagon, Robert is at home musing about the influence people can have on one another. "Henry has had an effect on me," he thinks. "After I got to know him, I didn't want his ginseng anymore. And I think I'm actually glad he didn't give in to me" (*Siege*, 140). He wonders if he has had any effect on Henry but decides that "anybody that old and set in his ways isn't going to be changed by anybody, much less a kid" (*Siege*, 142). But, as readers know, his effect on Henry has been monumental. Will Henry return to make amends with his wife and accept the consequences of his impulsive action 20 years ago? Though readers can only guess at the outcome, at the very least Henry will try for a life that reconciles his outer image with the person he would like to be. The gift of the ginseng root reinforces the story's ironic ending. Just when Robert has abandoned the idea of benefiting materially from his relationship with Henry, that is what happens: He is left with a $1,000 ginseng root that cannot possibly replace the friend who leaves. But Robert will discover Henry's absence and the gift in his mailbox only beyond the confines of this story, which ends with Robert musing, "I'm kind of glad to have Henry for a friend" (*Siege*, 142).

The reviews of this book were overwhelmingly positive, each reviewer singling out Hall's characterization of Robert and Henry. "You might not like Robert Short," writes *Kirkus*, "but Lynn Hall leaves you in no doubt as to how he got that way; though a little exaggerated in their open advocacy of a *caveat emptor* ethic, his parents are recognizable middle class types."[2] The *Kirkus* reviewer finds the evolving nature of the relationship between Robert and Henry predictable, but adds that the changes evinced in both characters "makes for an involving and sympathetic conclusion." In a *Booklist* review, *The Siege of Silent Henry* was described as "a perceptive story that depends more on characterization than action."[3] *Library Journal* agreed, noting that "characterization is excellent."[4]

Considerably less successful was Hall's portrayal of Carey and Ann, two 16-year-old girls who are the protagonists in *Flowers of Anger* (1976). In this book, their childhood friendship is put to the test when Ann is confronted by tragedy—a neighbor's deliberate shooting of Ann's beloved horse—and becomes consumed with revenge. As in *The Siege of Silent Henry*, strong characterization is required to give depth to the story, and without it, the book does not measure up to Hall's other work.

The story is told in the first person from Carey's point of view. As narrator, she becomes the more realistic of the two characters, while Ann's words and actions are filtered through the lens of Carey's friendship, which teeters on worship. Carey tries everything she can to help her friend Ann snap out of the depression that seizes her: She suggests activities; she tries tempting her back into life with a new horse; she even convinces a fellow Saddle Club member to ask Ann out on a date. But nothing works, and Ann continues to look for a way to get even with her neighbor, Mr. Greenawalt, for Nipper's death.

The larger problem is that Hall fails in her attempt to bring these two characters to life as 16-year-olds; sometimes their pursuits and conversations are on target for their age group, but an equal amount of time the two girls sound and act like preteens. Details that should serve to identify the characters as 16-year-olds—driving a car, wearing pantyhose—appear jarring instead. As in many of Hall's books, these teenage girls have not had much experience with boys, yet their conversations about them lack the intensity and concern present in comparable characters Hall created in the 1970s. Ann and Carey may have passed muster in the mid-1970s; to readers in subsequent decades, however, they can come across only as younger teenagers being masqueraded as older ones.

In truth, the basis for many of the activities that tie these friends together comes straight out of Hall's younger teenage years, when she was living in Webster City. She was 14 the year she bought Lady Bay, her first horse, and became best friends with a real-life Ann, owner of a horse named Taffy. During that year they did the things Hall writes about in this book: riding their horses to the drive-in movie, where they could watch the picture from outside the fence; scaring themselves silly on a moonlight ride mistaking a log in the river for a dead body. Ann's devotion to Taffy (who accompanied her to college and even, according to Hall, outlasted her marriage) no doubt served as the model for Hall's character Ann, and it is not hard to believe that a girl could love a horse the way the character loved Nipper. To be fair, Hall recounts some of these incidents in *Flowers of Anger* as having taken place when the girls were younger, and these scenes come alive in a way that those constructed in the present tense do not. But because it's hard to pinpoint just who these characters are now, readers have trouble becoming fully invested in their story.

Ultimately, the revenge Ann settles on is to destroy Mr. Greenawalt's rose garden, having determined that it is what he prizes most. Carey, who has tried her best to dissuade Ann from this plan, nonetheless lends her presence at this act of destruction as proof of her friendship. Because the book is told in flashback format, readers know from the beginning that Carey and Ann are still friends, although they never learn the consequences of Ann's act. At least that's how readers were probably meant to interpret this description of their friendship early in the book: "Whatever started it, it's grown over the last five years into something important. We know, now, how important. We found out last summer."[5]

Reader-response theorists posit that meaning resides in the mind of the reader rather than in the text, and a practical example of this theory can be found in comparing reviews of this book. In *Publishers Weekly*, the reviewer observed that "the girls' friendship is ruined as Anne refuses to be dissuaded from an act as base as Greenawalt's."[6] In contrast, the *Booklist* reviewer Denise Wilms stated that "despite her dislike of what Ann is about to do, [Carey] realizes that she values Ann's friendship too highly to cut her loose."[7] This latter reading is essential if the book is to be anything other than a questionable moral lesson: that people who commit wrongful acts do not deserve to have friends.

Does being a friend mean condoning a friend's behavior, right or wrong? This is a question that all young people face in their struggle to define the meaning of friendship, and one eminently worth posing in fiction. While it is the ultimate question in this book, it never quite reaches the surface in a denouement that seems facile. At one point in the last few pages of the story, Carey delivers a speech to Ann condemning her: "In case you're not aware of the fact, you have already lost your best friend. I used to look up to you, and want to be like you, and our friendship was one of the really good, important things in my life. And now I don't even like you anymore" (*Flowers*, 120). For the next few days, the girls have no contact; then, in an about-face, Carey arrives at Greenawalt's house just as Ann is about to commit her evil deed. She comes because she simply cannot stay away. "When I realized what you were turning into, I thought I could just trade you in on another friend, but I couldn't" (*Flowers*, 126). Carey's internal struggle has everything to do with her need to remain Ann's friend, even if it means becoming an accomplice to an act she despises. Ann obviously holds the power in this friendship.

But would they still be friends if they were on an equal footing? Judging from the story's beginning, their friendship is intact a year later, but in reality can it ever be the same? Such complex questions are not addressed, and a complicated situation is resolved too simply to make this book challenging.

If capturing the complexities involved in needing a friend proves too much for Hall in *Flowers of Anger*, she succeeds admirably at the same task in *Just One Friend* (1985). This book, written nine years later, is proof of Hall's maturing skill at conveying the motivations of her characters. Sixteen-year-old Dory Kjellings has been struggling through school, where she has been labeled a slow learner and even sent to a special school during sixth and seventh grades. She addresses her story to an imaginary friend: "You won't interrupt me, will you? Well, you can't very well, if I just made you up."[8]

Dory is from a midwestern farm town so small that it contains only five houses, strung out along the same side of the road and banded in front and back by fields of farm crops. Dory lives with her mother and five siblings in a rundown house at one end of the road; at the other end, in a neatly kept house, lives the town's only other child, Robin. Although they used to play together when they were little, Robin's abilities soon outstripped those of Dory, and they went in separate directions. Now, finally, Dory is being mainstreamed into eighth grade at the public school, and she is panicky: How will she know what to do and where to go? If only she had a friend to help her.

Dory's situation is familiar—almost everyone can recall growing up with someone who wasn't quite on track and who became the butt of other kids' jokes. Rarely, though, do we find these characters portrayed from their own perspectives. In *Just One Friend*, Dory explains how hard she tries, how she must read and reread passages before they have any meaning for her, how life sweeps by so fast that she can't keep up. We learn how difficult it is to keep trying in the face of continual failure and an unsupportive environment. Dory is propelled to persevere by the fear of becoming like her mother, whose days are so numbed by alcohol that she cannot run the household, much less look after her children. The family income consists of her mother's AFDC checks and her older brother's nightly excursions to hunt raccoons, whose pelts he can sell for up to $20 each.

In 1985, when this book was published, readers probably wouldn't have thought to make a causal connection between Dory's mental condition and her mother's drinking, unless they were to blame her slowness on a lack of proper attention at an early age. Thanks in large part to Michael Dorris's *The Broken Cord* (Harper and Row, 1989), however, society has developed a heightened awareness of fetal alcohol syndrome, which some current readers may associate with this story. Dory's description of her four-year-old brother, Bobby, is unsettling: "He hadn't started talking yet. I thought there was something wrong with him, but my mom didn't seem worried. He liked to be held a lot, and I liked having somebody to put my arms around" (*Friend*, 29). The social worker dispenses advice about nutrition but apparently hasn't observed Bobby closely enough to notice his arrested development.

Since she and Robin grew apart, Dory has not had a friend of her own. She keeps a careful eye on Robin's house and rushes over if she sees Robin outside training her dog. Then Dory knows she can be of help—she loves being a post, having to stand straight and not move while Robin and Jeckel make figure eights around her. Although Robin is kind to Dory, it's clear she doesn't see her as a friend; her best friend—the one she shares her secrets with—is Meredith, who lives on a nearby farm. Still, Dory takes comfort in knowing that Robin will be on the bus the first day of school to help her negotiate that scary first time.

Imagine Dory's shock, therefore, when Meredith drives up to Robin's house in her new birthday present, a car, and announces that this year she will be driving Robin to school. Dory is beside herself. First she asks Robin to ask Meredith if she can ride along; the answer is no. Then she asks her older brother Eldean if he will take her to school on the first day; again the answer is no. Finally, she concocts a plan to break up Robin and Meredith's friendship by planting the seeds of betrayal in each of them. She tells Meredith that Robin has called her boy-crazy, and she tells

Robin that Meredith thinks she acts like a little girl. The two friends almost fall for it—but in the middle of a tight-lipped conversation that is fast escalating into anger, Dory's name slips out, and they piece together her plot.

When this scheme doesn't work, Dory feels she has just one more chance, and that is to stop Meredith's car along the road before she gets to Robin's house. If she can cause Meredith to run into the ditch, Robin will have to take the bus with her. Unfortunately, that plan works all too well. Meredith is surprised indeed to see Dory standing in the middle of the road, and when she begins backing up to go around her, Dory rushes up, opens the door, and hits her. The car continues to back up into the ditch, where it stalls, motor running, and asphyxiates Meredith. But Dory doesn't find that out until later; she rushes to the bus stop, hoping the yellow bus will come before Meredith can recover control and come to take Robin away from her.

Meredith's death, delivered in the form of an afternoon announcement by the principal at school, comes as a shock to the reader as well as to Dory. While there's a hint on the first page of the story that Dory is feeling guilty about something, there's little reason to believe that it involves someone's death: "I didn't mean to do it to her. I would never do something that terrible. It was just, well, it was partly her fault. It was because of the car" (*Friend*, 1).

Dory's part in the tragedy sends her spiraling into a nervous breakdown. She is placed in the psychiatric ward of a nearby hospital, and when she improves she is sent to the State Training School for Girls. Previously, Dory had concocted a fantasy to keep her going: She would graduate from high school and become a waitress like the characters she saw on *Alice*, her favorite TV show. She'd earn money and get to eat at the restaurant. She'd make people happy by serving them food and chatting pleasantly. Ironically, her one selfish act makes this future possible. At the training school, she is finally in a situation where she can eat three good meals a day, bathe in hot water, wash her hair whenever she wants to, and learn at her own pace. Not surprisingly, having her basic needs met frees her to concentrate on her schoolwork and on developing social skills. Best of all, she tells us at the book's end, she finds a friend at the state school, someone who, like her, "never had a friend before." And with that, the story ends; it was, after all, being told to an imaginary friend, the reader, who is no longer needed in Dory's life.

Hall has done a remarkable job of creating Dory's voice—tentative and self-depreciating, but not to the point of annoying the reader or disengaging our empathy; complaining yet not whiny; logical in an often totally illogical way. As Patty Campbell observed in *Wilson Library Bulletin*, "To write from the perspective of a simple-minded person without writing a simple-minded book is a neat literary trick, and in *Just One Friend* Lynn Hall has pulled it off rather well."[9] Other reviewers agree. Writing in *Horn Book*, Mary M. Burns commented that "the use of the first person narrator is challenging, given her supposedly limited abilities, but Hall overcomes the difficulty with remarkable skill. The reader becomes the confidante that Dory always wanted—someone to listen without interrupting. As she pours out her anguish, she elicits genuine sympathy as well as understanding. Her naivete and her longing are deftly captured in tone and style, making a powerful statement about loneliness from the perspective of the outcast."[10] Li Stark, who reviewed this title for *School Library Journal*, noted that "so well does Hall capture Dory's feelings of isolation and desperate loneliness that readers who might think that 'dumb kids don't have feelings' are in for a rude awakening. Dory is a real and engaging person."[11] *Just One Friend* was chosen an ALA Best Book for Young Adults in 1985 and was issued in paperback by Collier Books in 1988.

An altogether different view of friendship is provided in *Where Have All the Tigers Gone?* (1989), a retrospective look at adolescent friendship by a 50-year-old woman returning to her hometown for a high school reunion (the odd thirty-second-year reunion is explained convincingly in the text). The book begins as Joanne Herne prepares to depart from home, and the life she describes at 50 sounds much like Hall's own life, transplanted from a rolling rural Iowa setting to a desert valley landscape in Arizona. Like Hall, Herne is a writer, but she writes westerns with such titles as *Badlands War* and *Rimrock Raiders*; though she is no Danielle Steele, her name is relatively well-known nationally.

The first two-thirds of the book consist of exposition, as the main character narrates what high school was like for her three decades ago. Part of this exposition comes in the form of a conversation with a friend, as they pore over her old yearbook and discuss some of the faces. "That one was my best friend," she says, pointing to a photograph of Charlotte Yoder. "We didn't have a thing in common."[12] The remaining exposition is in the form of reflection during her drive to the airport and the long plane ride across the country. The picture she paints is bleak: a girl thrust by her family's move to a new town in fifth grade who never quite reaches her stride in high school and doesn't understand why.

From her adult perspective, the main character muses about her old life: "Charlotte Yoder. Best friend. What an empty travesty of friendship that had been, compared with the depth and strength of friendships I'd known since. Charlotte and I had never connected at all. Why were we coupled in best-friend status all those years?" (*Tigers*, 13). One reason is that Charlotte was the first person Joanne met during those few vacant weeks of summer before school started, having been dragged home by Joanne's mother from the grocery store: "'I found you a new friend,' she said brightly. 'I was just over at Schultz's and I saw somebody who looked like she'd be about your age, so I invited her home to meet you'" (*Tigers*, 17). Joanne's response is shame: She was someone who couldn't even find her own friends. She asks Charlotte, somewhat rudely: "Did my mother really get you out of the store and drag you home, like you were a cabbage or something?" (*Tigers* 19). Charlotte, it turns out, is even more embarrassed than Joanne, but when school starts, she makes it clear that she and Joanne are friends. For her part, Joanne resists little and drifts easily into Charlotte's circle of friends.

Hall paints an often vivid portrait of Joanne Herne's school years, sketching in vignettes of some of the other students as Joanne remembers them. There's Roberto Rodriquez, always clowning and never giving the teacher the right answer; Alton

Grant, the heartthrob to whom Joanne is merely invisible; Patricia Winston, the beautiful, blond-haired snob; Bruce Whiteside, the shy "brain"; and Hazel Stott, the girl saddled with ugliness. Then there's Joanne's crowd of nondescript girls who are neither class leaders nor social rejects, hanging around together for lack of anyone else.

Not surprisingly, Joanne's take on these people turns out to have been faulty, as she learns 32 years later. Roberto is not at all dumb, but was simply doing what he could to fit his Mexican-American self into a majority culture. Alton Grant, whose status has plunged since high school, now proclaims to have "had the hots" for her long ago (even Joanne doesn't buy this). When she spies Bruce Whiteside, Joanne immediately blurts out that he was her first big love, and he confesses in turn that he also had a crush on her but wasn't able to act on it: "I just hadn't gotten to the point where I could talk to girls yet, and you scared the pants off me, you were so self-controlled" (*Tigers*, 111). Hazel Stott is the big surprise of the reunion, however, having been transformed from an ugly duckling into an elegant swan.

As for Joanne's "best friend," Charlotte is just the same, only happier. She has achieved what she wanted of life—marriage and a family—and even her husband's infidelities cannot mar her content. Joanne, who mentions offhand that their friendship in high school now seems so superficial, is taken aback when Charlotte responds: "I never thought of it that way. I thought we were very close back then. I don't think I've ever had a closer friend than you were" (*Tigers*, 115). In a particularly amusing sequence at the motel's pool, Charlotte asks Joanne about her life as a writer and then promptly falls asleep during Joanne's earnest, detailed answer.

It takes a basis of comparison to evaluate friendship, and the conversational exchange between Charlotte and Joanne can't really be appreciated by readers without that kind of hindsight. Most teenagers' eyes glaze over when their parents begin talking about old times. ("When I was your age" is a signal phrase.) A book based on a comparison of then and now isn't sufficient to compel their interest unless it also contains an exciting plot or likable characters that become real for them. In *Where Have All the Tigers Gone?* the anguish implicit in Joanne's adolescent disappointments doesn't come across to the reader, perhaps because the persona who tells the story is a 50-year-old woman for whom time has eased much of the pain. In addition, an entire eight years is telescoped into 95 pages, which necessarily forces the teller to gloss over details that might make the story seem more real. Yet this did not seem to bother reviewers, who felt that the story rang true and therefore had power (*Publishers Weekly*) and that it offered insights of value to adolescents (*School Library Journal*).

The part of the book that resonates most deeply is that set in the present, when the writer is at her reunion. This is, of course, precisely the part of the story that young people will not relate to. Teenagers may be able to fantasize their lives five or perhaps even 10 years into the future, but they simply cannot imagine themselves 32 years hence, as old as—maybe even older than—their parents. Even those who feel they are at the bottom of the heap socially will take little comfort in knowing that in 32 years the standings could be reversed and they may finally know what it's like to be admired by the same people who once ignored them.

Few reviewers questioned this book's appeal to Hall's usual young adult audience. The *School Library Journal* reviewer Judie Porter praised Hall's skill "at weaving teenage issues into this sensitive look at Herne's life" and calls the book "a deftly written nostalgic trip of one woman trying to piece together the progression from childhood to the adult world."[13] In contrast, *Publishers Weekly* emphasized that the very reason it rang true was that it was *not* a nostalgic view of the past but an objective view, and likened the book to "a message in a bottle to teenagers who may feel like outsiders in their own high schools."[14]

Interestingly, though, Joni Bodart wondered about the audience for this book and ended up writing two "booktalks" in *Wilson Library Bulletin*, one directed at young adults and the other at adults. To young adults, she asks, "Have you ever wondered what you'll be like years from now, who you'll be?" To adults, she puts the question differently: "Remember how you felt in high school, when everyone was prettier and more confident and smoother?" She tells young adult readers that they will discover a secret in this book: "no one sees you exactly as you see yourself." She urges adult readers to ignore the YA designation and remember that the book's narrator is from the class of 1955.[15]

Also concerned with the issue of appeal, Judith A. Sheriff gave this book to two young adult readers before writing her review for *Voice of Youth Advocates*. One put the book down after only three pages, while the other was intrigued by the premise, telling Sheriff that "her classmates are already curious about what they will be like at their ten-year reunion." While it is worthwhile for teenagers to see that time can turn them from losers into winners, she too questions "how many young adults will be interested in how thirty-two years of living might affect people."[16]

8. Sticks and Stones

The Siege of Silent Henry was one of two young adult novels by Lynn Hall to come out in 1972. The other was *Sticks and Stones*, also set in Buck Creek, Iowa, and also, like *Silent Henry*, about two people becoming friends. But there the similarity ends, because in *Sticks and Stones* Hall set out to write not just about friendship but about a friendship between a naive young man and a gay one, and not just about homosexuality but about society's response to it. Some of the same background characters in *Silent Henry* appear in *Sticks and Stones*, but the main characters are newly created. This book overshadowed much of her past work, receiving wider coverage and emerging as one of the most important books of that year. According to Alleen Pace Nilsen and Kenneth Donelson, *Sticks and Stones* was one of three landmark books that "opened the door to the treatment of homosexuality in books for young readers."[1] It was included among 29 honor books chosen by *English Journal* in 1972–1973 and was also named a Best Book for Young Adults by ALA's Young Adult Services Division in 1972.

Like any other subject that has long been taboo, homosexuality was often inappropriately given the spotlight when it finally did begin to appear in books for young people. The two other books Nilsen and Donelson cited as landmark books are John Donovan's *I'll Get There. It Better Be Worth the Trip* (Harper and Row, 1969) and Isabelle Holland's *The Man Without a Face* (Lippincott, 1972). Donovan's story depicts the trials of a 13-year-old boy thrust into a new life after his grandmother's death; an integral though not pivotal element of the story involves sexual experimentation between Davy and a male classmate, who has also recently experienced loss. In Holland's book, the growing friendship between 14-year-old Charles and the reclusive ex-teacher who tutors him loosens Charles's repressed emotions and stirs in him physical feelings toward the older man. Tied up in his confusion is the mystery of his own missing father, whose blurry face he sometimes sees in place of his tutor's disfigured one. Holland's theme, repeated throughout the book, has less to do with sexuality than with a boy's need for affection, and it focuses on the two-edged sword of freedom and responsibility.

Hall, too, uses the subject of homosexuality as a vehicle for exploring a larger theme. As Judy Blume has observed, *Sticks and Stones* isn't about homosexuality but about "injustice through the power of gossip."[2] Hall's emphasis is made clear by the title she chose for the book, taken from the familiar saying. But to claim that "words can never hurt me" is like whistling in the dark, a gesture of bravado in a situation over which one has no control.

In this book, Tom Naylor arrives in the picturesque village of Buck Creek from the more suburban Wheaton, Illinois, midway into his junior year. It's the town his mother grew up in, and after her divorce from Tom's father, she opts to return to familiar territory and open an antique shop. Tom has spent the summer helping his mother in the shop but has met few people his own age and none with whom he has anything in common. Early on, he made the mistake of being friendly to Floyd Scheffle, a somewhat dense young man who now continuously pesters him. Tom fervently hopes his social life will improve during his senior year, and there is no reason to think otherwise.

Shortly before school starts, Ward Alexander wanders into the shop, just back from the Air Force and renovating an old schoolhouse on his parents' farmland. Tom and Ward take an immediate liking to each other, and Tom is soon spending much of his free time helping Ward paint, sand, and hammer. In return, he is able to engage in the kind of easy conversation he has missed with someone who seems to value the same things—art, music, ideas. Hall's skill as a writer enables her to create two versions of the situation simultaneously: as it is seen by the townspeople, and as Tom sees it.

Ward's reappearance in town is accompanied by rumor: "Hey, I heard something today," says one of the town's inhabitants to Floyd Schleffe at the bait stand. "You remember Ward Alexander? He got discharged out of the Air Force. . . . They *say* he got a medical discharge." When Floyd is too slow to pick up on the innuendo, Orv explains further, "That kid's fruity, always was. Queer as a three dollar bill."[3] Floyd takes this in, lets it simmer a while, and then reasons that if Tom and Ward are friends, Tom must be queer too. This conclusion satisfies him, since it fixes the blame for his failure to win Tom's friendship on Tom rather than on his own deficiencies. Floyd can't wait to pass on the news. To ensure that this piece of gossip is taken seriously, he embellishes it, hinting that there was a reason he and Tom weren't friends: "All I can say is I wouldn't have a thing to do with Tom after—what happened" (*Sticks*, 61).

Buck Creek is a small town where being different—or even just an outsider—is an affront to the community. No one stops to question the rumor, but instead all use it to reaffirm their own place in Buck Creek. Amber, a local teenage girl who has hoped for Tom's attention, seizes on the rumor with particular relish. Soon Tom notices subtle differences in the way he is being treated in town and at school. He's puzzled that Karen, another music student whom he hoped to get to know better, never returns his glances, and he's upset when Mr. Harmon, the gym teacher, yells at him for putting his arm around Robert Short after a particularly competitive basketball game in which both boys have played well. All along, the readers "know" what the townspeople "know," but they also know what the townspeople don't: that not only is Tom not gay, but he is not even aware that Ward is gay. To describe Tom's responses in this situation, Hall writes that he feels as though he's in parentheses (*Sticks*, 107).

Is this lack of awareness realistic? Lynn Hall makes it so by setting her story in the insular community of Buck Creek, where people trust only those whose families they have grown up with. The rumor mill does not extend to Tom or his mother, even though she is part of a sewing circle and has begun dating a local dentist, an old classmate from a nearby town. Even Dr. Werle has heard and believes the rumor, and yet he keeps it from Tom's mother at the same time that he proposes to her. Several months pass before Tom finally learns of the situation from his high school principal, who informs him that he will not be allowed to perform at the state music finals because other parents have complained: They don't want their sons contaminated by sharing a room with him. Unable to imagine how a story like this could get started, he is full of self-doubts: "Do I look—different? Do I act funny, walk funny? My voice isn't high. Oh, God. Can they see something I don't see?" (*Sticks*, 149). When he pours out his feelings to Ward, Ward is full of sympathy but doesn't offer any solutions.

Much of the last half of the book recounts Tom's attempts to question his sexual identity. He covers the normal ground, reflecting on his attachment to his mother (Are they too close?), his love of music (Is he too sensitive?), and his track record with girls (Is it unnatural to care about their minds?). He makes a trip to the Dubuque library to research a paper for English but spends most of his time in the sociology stacks reading about homosexuality. None of the books, however, tells him what he really wants to know: "This is how you can tell whether or not you are one" (*Sticks*, 200). That Tom is probably not gay does not change this pattern of questioning; anyone who has had the slightest provocation to doubt his or her sexuality will relate to Tom's angst, no matter what end the self-questioning process leads to.

When Ward eventually reveals to Tom his own homosexual leanings and admits that his discharge was not because of asthma, as he previously stated, but resulted from being caught in a homosexual involvement, Tom is stunned. For months after the incident with the principal, Tom has taken solace in his friendship with Ward, oblivious to the fact that it's the very cause of his woes; the more time he spends with Ward, the more he exacerbates the problem and lends credibility to his detractors. Some of their conversations take on an ironic flavor in hindsight, such as

Ward's attempts to sound out Tom on the subject of homosexuality. He asks, "Does it bother you a whole lot—I mean, the idea that people are thinking you're homosexual? Is it revolting to you?" As part of his reply, Tom answers, "Sure it bothers me. Why wouldn't it? There are probably some very nice people who're that way, but I'm sure as hell not one of them" (*Sticks*, 147). Natural responses like this cause Ward to retreat further from the subject, but he eventually comes clean, with predictable results. He explains his needs as best he can, but Tom feels overwhelmingly betrayed and alone. Now he has no one.

Identity crises of this magnitude affect all of one's life, and Tom finds himself unable to concentrate in school. Without explaining the real reason he wants to leave, he writes to his father, hoping that he can finish out the term in Wheaton. His father tells him to stick it out and to visit in the summer. He makes a few futile gestures at asking out local girls to whom he would not have given the time of day before; one says she has to wash her hair, but the other gamely accompanies him to the Dairy Queen, her hair in rollers. He stops playing the piano; he stops caring about anything. Floyd Scheffle's ultimate triumph comes when he overhears the principal tell Tom that he is failing and will not graduate with the rest of his class. In Floyd's eyes, Tom has sunk down to his level, and when Tom leaves the school building that afternoon, he finds Floyd sitting in his car, waiting for a ride home.

The denouement comes in the form of a car accident they have that afternoon, an accident that kills Floyd and leaves Tom unconscious for three days, suffering broken bones but no permanent injuries. Tom knows his anger at Floyd prompted his reckless driving; he didn't want Floyd to die, but did he want to die himself? He is filled with self-recrimination but from the island of his hospital room begins to understand that he was a willing victim: "There was nothing wrong with me at all, until I started listening to their whispers" (*Sticks*, 219). In typical Lynn Hall fashion, the book ends on an ambiguous note as a visitor enters Tom's hospital room and Tom greets him: "Ward, I'm glad you came" (*Sticks*, 220).

"Among the avalanche of books for young adults that attempt to be relevant—to expose *all* the elements of life," declared *Publishers Weekly*, "'Sticks and Stones' stands apart, a fine example of quality writing and reading."[4] The reviewer for *School Library Journal*, however, offered a dissenting opinion, calling it "a bland fiction springing from an emotionally charged issue."[5]

In their discussion of *Sticks and Stones, I'll Get There. It Better Be Worth the Trip*, and *The Man Without a Face*, Nilson and Donelson pointed out that in all three books a death occurs. In Donovan's book, Davy's beloved dog is hit by a car while his father is having a "man-to-man" discussion with him about sex; in Holland's, the tutor has a fatal heart attack a month after Charles goes away to school. "In none of them can a direct cause-and-effect relationship be charted between the death and the homosexual behavior, but possibilities for blame are there." Critics of the time, they note, "were quick to object to the cumulative implications that the homosexual behavior will be punished with some dreadful event" (Nilsen and Donelson, 117).

Holland's book was made into a movie starring Mel Gibson in 1993, and even 20 years later, in a social climate ostensibly more hospitable to homosexuality, changes were made in the story that perpetuate the notion of homosexuality as a deviant and punishable behavior, a message that was clearly not part of Holland's book. Holland portrayed Charles as a young boy whose need for affection manifested itself in physical overtures toward his tutor, who had become a father figure as well as a friend. These intimations are totally missing from the film, which establishes both Charles and McLeod's credibility with the reader as heterosexual. In a passage that represents the turning point of their relationship in both the book and the movie, a distraught Charles comes to McLeod for help, and McLeod comforts him and puts him to bed. In the film viewers see nothing that would imply a sexual encounter, while in the book it's clear that something happens, though exactly what is not spelled out for the reader (presumably, the physical closeness to his tutor triggers in Charles an erection and possibly ejaculation). The screenplay was rewritten so that the local police officer, already suspicious of McLeod because of his reclusive nature, sees Charles coming downstairs in his underwear and jumps to conclusions; the tutor is banished from the community by self-righteous people who erroneously assume sexual molestation. While the satisfaction for readers is found in Charles's growth when months later his life takes shape and he puts the summer's events into perspective, the impact for the film audience resides in the injustice of the story's resolution as homosexual behavior that did not occur is nonetheless punished. In that way, the message of the film becomes much closer to Hall's book than it is to Holland's.

Unlike the final version of *Sticks and Stones*, Hall's original manuscript included no kind of retribution, intentional or inferred, for any of the characters. The story Hall submitted ended with Tom's decision to leave Buck Creek after the principal has told him that he would not be graduating.[6] The town has beat him, he feels, and he sees no recourse but to take his savings of $500 and start anew elsewhere; he'll let his mother know after he has left, and he realizes that her new life will ease the pain of his leaving. He does not renew contact with Ward, but neither does he condemn him.

When Sandy Griefenstein, Hall's editor at Follett, acquired this manuscript, she knew it would be controversial and was excited at the prospect. But shortly before the book went to press, it caught the attention of upper management, who insisted that its ending be revised. They would not publish a book that appeared to condone a homosexual relationship. Hall proffered an alternative ending in which Tom takes a more active role in shaping his life in Buck Creek. He becomes a mediator, in effect, making amends with Ward (who has just sold his first book) but at the same time deciding to invite Meredith to a party he is planning in Ward's honor. Thus he signals his intention to choose friends on his own terms rather than the terms of the community, and he reinforces for readers his own heterosexual stance. Although less ambiguous about Tom's sexuality than either the first or the final ending, this ending also spells out an acceptance of homosexuality as an alternative lifestyle. Perhaps that's the reason it, too, was rejected in favor of the more dramatic conclusion that featured Tom's car accident. Hall has since regretted her compromise, though in retrospect the original ending feels weak compared with the story's other strengths. *Booklist* found the ending "abrupt and somewhat unsatisfactory" while praising the "involving" story and Hall's "convincing" characterizations.[7]

While *Sticks and Stones* is certainly not Tom's coming-out story, the ending as published respects his right to determine his own sexual orientation and to choose his own friends. One of the book's strengths is that Hall feels no need to prove that Tom is "normal" or to conclude the story by integrating him into the social fabric of Buck Creek. There is no overt mention, as in the second draft, of Tom's desire to date, although textual clues on the last few pages point to an affirmation of his heterosexuality, giving him the freedom to once again be friends with Ward. But readers who choose to can just as easily read the ending as one step on a road to discovery, wherever it may lead; this reading seems to be favored by letters Hall has received from gay male readers.

After the book's publication, Lynn Hall received numerous letters from readers expressing their gratitude for her having written "about them."[8] One student, pursuing his master's degree in English, wrote: "Perhaps, when I was seventeen, the thing I could have used most was your novel—not so much to lead me out of the proverbial closet—but to allow me to understand that difference is not always deviance." Another writer wrote to tell Hall that *Sticks and Stones* was "one of the best novels—maybe the best novel—containing gay characters I've ever read. No taint at all of 'compassion' for us gays; instead a fine feeling for love in the abstract and the value of friendship. . . . It would be great if your book was in every high school library. I'm in my 20's now and have already gone through what Tom went through. But, God, a book like yours would have been so welcome at the time." This writer mentioned that he had just happened to run across the book at the public library. Another writer stated that Hall's novel is "worthy I thought for a high school English class to dissect, if only our society weren't so afraid."

Hall captures at once the homophobia that pervades closed communities and the paranoia it can engender. Through the character of Ward, she demonstrates that not all gay men look alike; that they cannot be distinguished by a voice, a walk, a particular type of movement; that the inclination to be homosexual is based on emotional needs as much as on physical ones. And through the character of Tom, she demonstrates that questions about sexual identity are universal.

While young readers' awareness of homosexuality has broadened since *Sticks and Stones* came out, the homophobia exhibited by the townspeople of Buck Creek has not disappeared. In that respect, the story remains believable. Readers today, however, might find Tom's extreme naiveté hard to swallow unless they are reminded that he lived in a world without MTV and *Saturday Night Live*, venues that frequently depend on homosexuality for their humor. Yet the core of Hall's book speaks so directly to the issues at hand that the text does not come across as dated, except in brief situations where Ward expounds on the use of profanity, explaining why he says "summer ditch" rather than "son of a bitch." Such language, perhaps still of concern to parents who see it in print, no longer fazes the average teenager. As out of place as it might seem, this element also supports the theme, as Ward is trying to master the power of words in his effort to become an accomplished writer.

The childhood verse to which the title refers is introduced in the text when Tom attempts to cheer up a seven-year-old boy whose older brothers have been picking on him. Its use is ironic at this point in the story, since at the same time that Tom is innocently reciting the singsongy words, readers are aware that the townspeople are busy fueling the rumors about him. Yet the title can be read both ironically and straightforwardly. The townspeople's gossip *has* hurt Tom (who has actually suffered broken bones as an indirect result), but in coming to terms with his accident he is determined to abide by his own advice in the future: He will no longer let his own actions be influenced by what others say or think.

Sticks and Stones has been out of print since the early 1980s, a casualty of Follett's having closed down its trade publishing operations. It was picked up by Dell and published in paperback in

1977, but that edition, too, is out of print. Film rights, however, have been under option to the same independent filmmaker for at least a decade. Judging from the alterations made to *The Man Without a Face*, Hall's story is right on target for a contemporary audience. Periodically, Hall receives a call from the filmmaker reporting on his progress in procuring funding to make the film. Often, it seems as if the project will become a reality, but in the film industry, as anywhere else, success depends on the timely conjunction of the right idea with the right people.

9. Mystery and Suspense

Mysteries have always been considered a good way to entice non-readers and reluctant readers, but avid readers, too, love to be absorbed by a good mystery. As Zena Sutherland observes in *Children and Books*, today's young readers, nurtured on television and comic books, are used to fast-moving plots and lots of action.[1] And what can be more satisfying for young readers than identifying with someone their own age who is capable of routinely outwitting the collection of adults who surround them?

Although she is seldom associated with this genre, a respectable portion of Lynn Hall's 80-plus books have been mystery stories, many for intermediate readers and four of them for young adults. A longtime mystery fan, Hall has absorbed many of the basic criteria for creating suspense and credibility. Her plots are logically developed, and for careful readers she offers clues along the way. The mysteries her young characters find themselves embroiled in are often drawn from everyday life, and, likewise, her characters are ordinary people caught up in extraordinary circumstances. There are no Nancy Drews here; her characters are more likely to drive a beat-up VW bug than a red sports car, if they drive at all, and they are more likely to be encountering their adventures in their own neighborhoods than on a trip abroad. In large part, Hall's success in creating a good mystery rests on her strength of characterization. Her fully developed young people win readers' confidence as they cope with adventure and danger.

From the time of her second book, *The Secret of Stonehouse* (1968), Lynn Hall has consistently written mystery stories. Most of these books, however, have been for middle-grade and younger readers. In the late 1970s and early 1980s, Hall wrote a series of mystery stories for upper elementary readers, published by Garrard. *The Mystery of Pony Hollow* (1978) was the first of these books. Set on a farm in rural Iowa, it is the tale of Sarah, who in exploring the woods on the farm her family has just bought discovers an old shed and, in it, the skeleton of a horse. Her curiosity about how it got there and why prompts her to do some investigating into the past, and she successfully pieces together the history of her new home. These books are entertaining mysteries in which young people use their heads, and often exhibit a bit of spunk, to solve puzzles. Several of these early books, first published by Garrard and advertised for ages eight to 12, have been reissued by Random House in their Stepping Stone series for ages seven to nine.

The Mystery of the Lost and Found Hound (1979) involves an interstate dog-stealing business, brought to a halt by a young girl who finds one of the stolen puppies and is clever enough to trace it to its owner. Hall based a much later book, *The Tormentors* (1990), on a similar theme but created a longer and more elaborate story and changed the situation into one in which a young boy's dog is stolen. Interestingly, both books were advertised by the publishers for ages eight to 12, but the earlier book is liberally illustrated and has a much younger appeal; *The Tormentors* is straight text and takes the format of a chapter book. The books also differ in the level of adventure and risk the main characters are exposed to. While the girl in *The Mystery of the Lost and Found Hound* has a brush with danger when she hides in a vanload of dogs, she is undiscovered. The main character in *The Tormentors* is kidnapped by the dognappers, although he escapes before he sustains any real harm. *The Tormentors* received a mixed reception from reviewers, praised as "exciting," "smoothly written and nicely paced," and "plausible" by *School Library Journal*, and panned by *Voice of Youth Advocates* as reading "like a homework assignment performed by an unwilling pupil."[2]

In general, Hall has made her mysteries for preteens suspenseful without exposing the young people in them to physical danger. Her young adult mysteries, however, go beyond suspense to involve the characters in compelling and often-perilous situations. After at least a dozen mysteries for preteen readers, Hall's first YA mystery came out in 1987. *Ride a Dark Horse* was issued by Morrow in hardcover, with a simultaneous edition in paperback from Avon. A topnotch mystery set in the world of horse racing, it reads like a Dick Francis book and was planned as the first of a series. Not surprisingly, Hall is a big Dick Francis fan, and his books line her shelves at home. Like Francis, she fashions a plot for *Ride a Dark Horse* that turns on a knowledge of horse racing and breeding, and she deftly includes all the requisite elements—danger, deceit, and daring. Seventeen-year-old Gusty McCaw finds herself in an untenable position when she is fired for something she didn't do. She soon figures out that she has stumbled on a secret that someone would kill—perhaps *has* killed—to keep, and the only way she can unravel the mystery is to place herself deeper and deeper in danger.

McCaw, like Francis's lead characters, is resourceful without being unrealistic. Gusty and her father are part of the entourage that works at Tradition Farm, where racing horses are trained and bred. Until his freak accidental death three months previously, her father was in charge of weanlings and yearlings, and Gusty herself works as an exercise rider there. When by chance she notices a strange occurrence in the breeding shed late one night, she is motivated to investigate. Suddenly, within days, she is framed for theft and is dismissed from Tradition Farm. Her desire to clear her own name and get to the bottom of her father's death sends her on an undercover adventure in which she, like the best of Francis's protagonists, ends up fighting for her own life. The action is fast-paced, and readers are able to figure out enough of the mystery to keep them satisfied while remaining in suspense about how it will all turn out. The mystery itself is elaborate, involving a substitution of a look-alike horse for a Kentucky Derby winner; the plot is well-constructed, with no loose ends that niggle. The *School Library Journal* reviewer Louise L. Sherman found this book an exciting and satisfying read: "The villains are villainous and the danger [is] sometimes terrifying."[3] Kim Sleeper, the reviewer for *VOYA*, was enthusiastic enough to proclaim this book "a definite winner," and noted that "YAs will look forward to the future adventures of Gusty McCaw."[4]

The next YA mystery Hall wrote presents a completely different character and setting. *A Killing Freeze* (1988), also published in hardcover by Morrow and in paperback by Avon, is set in a small Minnesota town during the four days of the town's annual Winter Fest. The main character, Clarie, lives with her father, who has raised her alone since infancy. They depend on a snowmobile dealership for their income, and the annual festival, filled with ski, snowmobile, and sledding races, always provides their business with a much-needed income and momentum to sustain it over the year. This year, however, death disrupts the Fest, with the first victim being Clarie's kind older neighbor, Mrs. Ameling, who lives outside of town on the lot adjacent to theirs. Clarie is the one to find her, and she immediately calls the sheriff. The investigation proceeds along with the Fest, which Clarie's dad runs. A second body is found the following day; this time the victim is an ice-sculpture contestant. The town is abuzz, and as Clarie helps her father with errands—delivering trophies, finding volunteers to officiate at the races, and overall troubleshooting—she sorts through the snippets of information she has learned.

It is often true that solutions come when we are not looking directly at the problem but have been distracted from it, and such is the case here. Clarie has all the pieces but can't put them together until she happens to be looking at a young participant, bundled in a snowsuit, whom she takes for a boy until his hat is removed. Then it hits her: The face she has been trying to place belongs to a woman, not a man, and she knows who the killer is. Unfortunately, the killer is present, too, and witnesses the dawning of recognition as Clarie's eyes fall on her. The chase is on, and suspense builds quickly toward the climax, when the sheriff and Clarie's dad arrive in time to save her.

Hall deftly plants enough supporting evidence early on to justify the unexpected ending. The backdrop of the Winter Fest is a panorama of activities and people in which several alternative possibilities are presented, allowing the reader to develop and discard "whodunit" theories along the way. While there is considerably less adventure and action in *A Killing Freeze* than in *Ride a Dark Horse*, the strong suit here is Clarie's thought process. Reviewing for *School Library Journal*, Susan F. Marcus praised Hall's work: "Suspense is written skillfully into short, dramatic chapters."[5] The *VOYA* reviewer Delia A. Culberson suggested that "while the younger crowd will like the spunky heroine and suspenseful plot, older teens will find the narrative simplistic and the resolution unconvincing."[6] Both reviewers noted the skill with which Hall presented the rugged winter setting, in Marcus's words, "sometimes-thrilling, sometimes-chilling."

In *Murder at the Spaniel Show* (1988), Hall creates another realistic, bustling backdrop for murder, here parlaying her extensive knowledge of the dog show world into a readable, suspenseful mystery novel. Tabitha Trost, "Tabby" for short, is another one of Hall's female characters who are thoroughly enamored of animals. Tabby's love for dogs has led her to decide she wants to make a life's work out of breeding and showing dogs, and she wastes no time in preparing herself. The summer before her junior year in high school, she lands a job (after painstakingly searching out leads at dog shows and veterinarians' offices, much as Hall herself did) at Quintessence, an upscale kennel specializing in springer spaniels and housed on a Connecticut country estate. The story takes place during the weekend of the eighty-ninth annual National English Springer Spaniel Specialty Show, being hosted at Quintessence. Breeders and trainers from across the country have descended on the grounds, and the cast of characters is a microcosm of the dog show world. Competition for wins is fierce, since a win can mean thousands of dollars in future stud fees and dog sales. Because judges favor different criteria—a dog's conformation, for instance, over its movement—the choice of judges can be crucial, and this year's judge is Ted Quinn, the estranged twin brother of the owner of Quintessence, Turner Quinn. When mysterious notes appear threatening Ted Quinn's life if he judges the best in show, the local police are brought in. Any one of a number of dog owners or trainers has a motive for wanting Ted Quinn out of the picture, and Tabby, along with the police detective, considers them in turn.

Hall's characterization of Tabby is first-rate as she creates a teenager who notices details around her and strains to find meaning in what she sees, hears, and knows. Mary Hedge, the reviewer for *VOYA*, called Tabby "a well-described character who is easy to like and identify with because she is an average teenager with no special problems or abilities. . . . Her courage and cleverness are inspiring."[7] The dog show environment is portrayed vividly enough that readers feel they are walking through the grounds alongside Tabby. As in many mysteries of this sort, a few red herrings are offered to throw readers off course, but by the time of the resolution all pieces of the puzzle fall into place, and motives are clear. Tabby's boss, Turner Quinn himself, turns out to be the guilty one, and although the modus operandi of the murder is unusual, it is to Hall's credit that it is still believable. *School Library Journal*'s reviewer for this book, Judy Greenfield, was enthusiastic in her praise: "The details of the dog show add interest and atmosphere in this well-written and well-paced mystery. Most of all, the heroine speaks with the convincing voice of someone caught up in a terrifying conflict. She really admires and trusts Turner. Gradually, she and readers realize how menacing he is. Turner's death in jail, of a heart attack, like the one he has caused his hated twin, adds an ironic twist. Young adults will certainly enjoy this much better-than-average entry."[8]

Murder in a Pig's Eye (1990) marks a stylistic departure for Lynn Hall. The tone is breezy and lighthearted, at times tongue-in-cheek. Sixteen-year-old Bodie Tureen lives with his parents and sister in a small New Hampshire village, where his father is pursuing his dream of the good life: publishing a small weekly newspaper. Bodie is on the brink of manhood, and he consistently checks his body to see how it's coming along. So far, he's avoided acne but still carries a small roll of fat around his middle. Part of the reason he agrees to take a temporary job helping a neighbor, Henry Siler, with farm chores—Siler has injured his arm and his wife is away—is that he thinks the work will make him lean and strong. Bodie envisions his manly self, right down to the plaid shirt he'll be wearing, being "discovered" by a beautiful teenage girl.

Henry Siler is a man of few words, but Bodie quickly gets into the swing of the chores—feeding Gloria, the prize pig; gathering eggs from the chickens; cutting and stacking firewood. His job is made more pleasant by the absence of Bella Siler, who has a reputation for ruling Henry—and everything else in sight—with an iron fist. A couple of chance remarks start Bodie wondering where Bella has gone, and when he asks, Henry refuses to say. In idle conversation one day, Bodie, his sister, and his friend Zach consider the possibility of foul play: Could Henry have murdered Bella and hidden her somewhere on the farm? "'Nah,' said Bodie, 'that doesn't happen in real life.' 'In a pig's eye it doesn't,' Zach snorted."[9] Bodie has a hard time shaking the idea, though, and he finds himself looking for evidence as he works around the farm. Studying Henry's behavior closely only confirms his suspicions. His task becomes one of finding Bella's body without drawing Henry's attention in the process. Hall deftly blends suspense with comedy as each of Bodie's attempts is foiled, often in ways verging on slapstick. Ultimately he does find her body, but, as his sister wryly says, "she was still using it."

Hall's mastery of language, timing, and humor shines here. Gloria the pig is described as having a body that "was smooth and as firmly packed as the sausages that were her ultimate destiny" (*Pig's Eye*, 8). Her feed is called Sow Joy, and the village is named Lower Bacpane. Bodie's imagination is fueled by the mysteries that he reads, and at one point he projects himself into a future where, after having solved this crime, he will be living in a Boston penthouse and solving other crimes with the help of a legman named Archie. Rex Stout fans will recognize the allusion to Nero Wolfe, the fictional detective who weighs a seventh of a ton. Amusing details sharpen the descriptions and characterizations. The Silers' kitchen clock is shaped like a frying pan. Bodie's father, who used to work as a pressman for the *Boston Globe*, reads the evening *Globe* "in search of typo errors that wouldn't have occurred if he were still working in the pressrooms" (*Pig's Eye*, 35).

Hall has written this book with the confidence of a mature writer, but not all reviewers reacted to it in the same way. Beth E. Anderson, writing in *VOYA*, was obviously expecting something else when she picked up the book to read, and she did not recommend it to *VOYA* readers. "Hall is an award-winning YA author," she wrote, "and yet *Murder in a Pig's Eye* reads as if it were written during a boring weekend. It was a chore reading it to the end."[10] Doris A. Fong, on the other hand, called it "warm, well written, and genuinely funny" in her review for *School Library Journal*."[11] "This wry novel," she added, "combines full characterization and wacky situations to keep readers chuckling." Stephanie Zvirin was just as enthusiastic about it in her *Booklist* review, although her emphasis was different from Fong's: "It's wacky plot, not oddball characterization, that Lynn Hall depends on in her broadly sketched comedy-mystery, which takes cues from both the Hardy Boys and the Three Stooges. . . . What the author lacks in genre background and comic timing, she makes up for by revitalizing a whodunit formula with a good dose of entertaining silliness."[12]

Hall has shown a facility for writing young adult mysteries, and the four that have been published have met with critical success and sold moderately well. *Ride a Dark Horse* was billed as "a Gusty McCaw mystery," the implication being that it was the first of a series. Indeed, at the end of the book, Gusty is poised for further adventures, having been hired by the Jockey Club's security division. Her knowledge of horses and her experience as a stable hand and rider put her in a perfect position to investigate rumors and gather information. In Gusty, Hall created a likable character who could hold her own, just the kind of protagonist mystery readers love. Yet anyone who reads *Ride a Dark Horse* and goes in search of Gusty's next adventure will be disappointed. The real mystery here is why there were no more Gusty McCaw books.

In fact, there is a sequel, but it has remained unpublished. According to Hall, the publishers with whom she contracted for the book, Avon and Morrow, changed their marketing strategy and decided not to continue the series. By that point, she was already midway into writing the second book, and so she finished it. The manuscript is caught in limbo. Understandably, no publisher has been willing to take the second book in a series when it does not have the first. This is an aspect of publishing over which readers—and authors—have frustratingly little control.

10. A Life's Work

Lynn Hall's career as a writer for young adults parallels the rise of the realistic novel in young adult literature. Her first book, *The Shy Ones*, came out in 1967, the same year that saw the publication of S. E. Hinton's *The Outsiders*. Hall's book recalls similar stories prevalent in the 1950s and 1960s, though it is not as saccharine. *The Outsiders*, however, represented a radical change in focus, speaking to a segment of the teenage population who had never before seen themselves reflected in the literature supposedly aimed at them.

Soon other authors, including Hall, turned their efforts toward providing realistic portrayals of the challenges faced by young people. Many of the young adult books Hall wrote during the 1970s and 1980s fall into the category of problem novels, books that deal with an adolescent's struggle for identity and acceptance in light of contemporary societal concerns. In *Sticks and Stones* the issue is homosexuality; in *Halsey's Pride*, epilepsy; in *Just One Friend*, learning disabilities and alcoholism. Dysfunctional families, as we've seen, are rampant in her books. Altogether, Hall has written over 80 titles, 25 of which are young adult novels. With the exception of three young adult books published by Follett, most if not all her YA novels are still in print, and four are also available in paperback. In fact, at times Hall has been accused of being too prolific.

Why do some writers become well-known names in the literary field while others do not? Although reviews of Hall's books can be mixed, she has received her share of praise from critics. Five of her books have been ALA Best Books, one is a Golden Kite Award Winner, and one is the winner of a Boston Globe–Horn Book Award. Certainly the quality of a writer's work is a big factor,

Lynn (right) with her sister Jan in 1985.

and quantity can also play a role. But beyond the work of writers are other decisive elements: editors who generate in-house enthusiasm for a book; publishers who have both the means and the commitment to stand behind a book or an author with promotional dollars; and writers themselves, who willingly devote time and preparation to speaking engagements and school visits. Finally, there is serendipity—the unpredictable intersection of a book's publication with a receptive market.

In several ways, Lynn Hall's publication history has worked against her. Her 13-year association with Follett, with whom she published a total of 26 books, ended when that publisher closed its doors; so, too, did Garrard cease its publishing activities with 13 of her titles on its list. The irony of losing her two publishers almost simultaneously was not lost on Hall: "I don't think it was my fault," she jokingly remarked at the time. Although fortunately she had already placed *The Leaving* with Scribner's, the situation nonetheless had an adverse impact on her career: Within a short time it rendered all her backlist titles unavailable for purchase. The rights to these books reverted to her, and only recently has she resold several of the Garrard titles to Random House. But books like *Sticks and Stones* and *Too Near the Sun*, both of which are suited to contemporary adolescent readers and are every bit as readable as many of the books being heralded today, scarcely can be found.

Since 1980, Hall's books have been published primarily by Scribner's, although for a time she had an agent who also placed books with Morrow and Harcourt Brace. Her relationship with Scribner's got off to a wonderful start with *The Leaving*, which was an ALA notable book as well as a winner of the Boston Globe–Horn Book Award. During the decade of the 1980s, there was every indication that Hall would achieve significant status as a young adult author, but major prizes have eluded her.

Because Hall had worked with so many different editors at Follett, she was elated when she finally landed in what she saw as a stable and nurturing author-editor relationship. But shortly after *The Leaving* was published, the editor who had acquired it left Scribner's as part of a corporate downsizing and Clare Costello moved up to take her place. Does the way in which writer and editor come together influence a writer's career? Perhaps not, yet authors often fare best with the editors who have "discovered" them. That was certainly true of Hall's relationship with Sandy Griefenstein of Follett, whom she thought of as a friend as well as an editor. Much later, Hall came to feel that way about Diane D'Andrade at Harcourt Brace. Hall originally had a different editor at Harcourt Brace with whom she worked on the Zelda books, a series for younger readers.

Like Costello, D'Andrade inherited Hall when she was promoted to a different position within the company. From the beginning, however, D'Andrade expressed enthusiasm for Hall's previous work and excitement at working with her. Although they never met in person, their working relationship was friendly and productive. Among the books D'Andrade acquired was *Flying Changes*, which Costello had rejected several years before. On the other hand, Hall feels that despite working together on some two dozen books, she and Costello never got past the formal stage. In early 1992, Hall wrote letters to Costello and D'Andrade to announce that she was taking a break from writing. She received a polite note of regret from Costello, while D'Andrade called her immediately, urging her to reconsider.

To borrow a term from the world of adult publishing, most of the books Hall published with Scribner's were treated as *midlist* books, titles that a publisher sends out to the market with average publicity—catalog coverage, the standard review copies, and perhaps a press release—but without any extra push. A memorable exception was *The Solitary*, which had the kind of in-house support that distinguishes it from the rest of a list. For years, Maureen Hayes was Scribner's school and library promotions director. A dynamic and highly respected individual, she considered *The Solitary* Hall's strongest book to date, and she promoted it in the best way possible—by word of mouth. That book was an ALA Best book for Young Adults and a Golden Kite winner; it was also quickly picked up by Bantam for publication in paperback.

Another way in which editors make a significant difference is the amount of editorial direction and support they provide. Mary Stolz, a prolific and respected writer who for years worked with Ursula Nordstrom at Harper and Row, recalls how Nordstrom would mark certain passages of her manuscripts with the notation "NGEFY," which meant "Not good enough for you." Although Costello didn't prod Hall to excellence in the same way, Hall was satisfied with the editorial attention she received from her editor at Scribner's. Costello sometimes suggested major changes—strengthening a character, for instance—that she felt would improve Hall's stories, but she left line changes to the hand of the copy editor.

Oddly enough, the editor who made the most difference in Hall's life was someone she never had the chance to work with. Shortly before Follett quit publishing trade books, it hired Ellen Rudin to fill the spot staffed by the succession of editors who followed in Griefenstein's wake. Before she joined Follett, Rudin was already aware of Hall's work; furthermore, Rudin told Hall that her writing talent had been underutilized and that the chance to work with Hall was a primary factor in Rudin's taking the job at Follett. Motivated by this editor's faith in her, Hall promptly set about writing the best book she could; it was for Rudin that Hall wrote *The Leaving*. As luck would have it, Follett closed down its trade publishing department shortly thereafter, leaving Rudin out of a job and unable to publish the book. For a while, both editor and author harbored the hope that Rudin would land elsewhere and bring the book out; when that didn't happen, Hall finally submitted it to Scribner's.

Whereas Follett had treated Hall as one of its top authors, taking her to several ALA annual conferences, at Scribner's she became a little fish in a big pond. From time to time the publisher invited her to nearby regional meetings, but she didn't enjoy the same opportunities for exposure that she had known at Follett. In some districts where her books were popular, schools and libraries sought her out, and for several years Hall maintained an active schedule of speaking and writing. In 1990, she spoke to about 20 different groups; since then, her dog breeding business has become a larger part of her life and livelihood, and it is harder for her to leave home for periods longer than a weekend at a time.

With so many of her older books out of print, Hall set out a few years ago to start a small publishing company to republish selected titles for which she held the rights. Her intention was to sell these books when she traveled to dog shows, which she has been doing with growing frequency. To her dismay, however, she found that books didn't sell particularly well at these shows, and so she contacted the major bookstore chains in hopes they would carry them. Again she had no luck—the chains explained that they didn't deal with small presses directly. One buyer, however, loved the books and passed them on to Random House, promising that if Random House published them, the chain would guarantee a large order. Thus several of Hall's early books for younger readers have recently been reissued in Random House's Stepping Stones series, directed at primary-grade readers.

Not long ago Lynn Hall was the keynote speaker at a young writer's conference, where her message was designed to inspire her listeners: If you're willing to work hard, you can achieve your dreams, she told them. Using her own life as an example, she described herself as an ordinary student and a girl not particularly pretty in high school (an asset which was then almost a prerequisite for popularity). Yet she had a vision of the life she wanted for herself—a life that included animals and plenty of space. "I ended up with the life I wanted," she told her young audience, "because I did what was necessary to get there."

Above all, Lynn Hall is practical. These days, she takes pleasure in the life she leads and dwells neither on what might have been nor what might be to come.

Notes and References

Chapter 1

1. Hall, Lynn, *Tazo and Me* (New York: Scribner, 1985), 14; hereafter cited in text as *Tazo*.
2. Hall, Lynn, *Something About the Author: Autobiography Series*, vol. 4 (Detroit: Gale Research, 1987), 195; hereafter cited in text as *SAAS*.

Chapter 2

1. Hall, Lynn, *Lynn Hall's Dog Stories* (Chicago: Follett, 1972), 24.
2. Hall, Lynn, *Where Have All the Tigers Gone?* (New York: Scribner, 1989), 10; hereafter cited in text as *Tigers*.
3. Hall, Lynn, *Careers for Dog Lovers* (Chicago: Follett, 1978), 10; hereafter cited in text as *Careers*.

Chapter 3

1. Letter dated 16 February 1966, held in Kerlan Collection, University of Minnesota, Minneapolis, M.F. 393.
2. Letter dated 19 May 1967, held in Kerlan Collection, M.F. 393.
3. *Booklist*, 15 February 1968, 699.
4. Gregory, Agnes, *Library Journal*, 15 January 1968, 304.
5. *Booklist*, 1 January 1969, 496.

Chapter 4

1. Hall, Lynn, *Too Near the Sun* (Chicago: Follett, 1970), 189; hereafter cited in text as *Sun*.
2. Hall, Lynn, *The Leaving* (New York: Scribner, 1980), 7; hereafter cited in text as *Leaving*.
3. Manuscript notes held in Kerlan Collection, M.F. 393.
4. Estes, Sally, *Booklist*, 1 October 1980, 206.
5. Hall, Lynn, *The Solitary* (New York: Scribner, 1986), 34; hereafter cited in text as *Solitary*.
6. Zvirin, Stephanie, *Booklist*, 15 November 1986, 502.
7. Butler, Judy M., *School Library Journal* (January 1987), 82.
8. Hall, Lynn, *Flyaway* (New York: Scribner, 1987), 55.
9. Ojibway, Mary, *Voice of Youth Advocates* (*VOYA*; December 1987), 235.
10. *Publishers Weekly*, 25 September 1987, 112.
11. Personal interview with Lynn Hall at Touchwood, Elkader, Iowa, 28 July 1992; all quotes not otherwise attributed derive from this interview or from subsequent phone calls.

Chapter 5

1. Wood, Catherine, *School Library Journal* (November 1983), 92.
2. Hand, Dorcas, *Horn Book* (October 1983), 582.
3. Wilms, Denise M., *Booklist*, 15 September 1983, 171.
4. Hall, Lynn, *Halsey's Pride* (New York: Scribner, 1990), 49; hereafter cited in text as *Halsey*.
5. Meisner, Sylvia V., *School Library Journal* (April 1990), 140.
6. Pickworth, Hanna, *ALAN Review* (Fall 1991).
7. Wilms, Denise M., *Booklist*, 15 April 1987, 1289.
8. Dean, Beth Wheeler, *Voice of Youth Advocates* (June 1987), 78.
9. *Publishers Weekly*, 27 June 1986, 95.

10. Peasley, Rosie, *Voice of Youth Advocates* (August–October 1986), 144.
11. Rochman, Hazel, *Booklist*, 1 June 1986, 1454.
12. Hall, Lynn, *Half the Battle* (New York: Scribner, 1982), 13; hereafter cited in text as *Half*.
13. Harris, Karen, *School Library Journal* (August 1982), 126.
14. Chelton, Mary K., *Voice of Youth Advocates* (August 1982), 31.
15. Zvirin, Stephanie, *Booklist*, 1 May 1982, 1153.
16. *Publishers Weekly*, 12 March 1982, 85.

Chapter 6

1. Nelms, Beth, Ben Nelms, and Linda Horton, "A Brief But Troubled Season: Problems in YA Fiction," *English Journal* (January 1985), 93.
2. Zvirin, Stephanie, *Booklist*, 1 April 1984, 1110.
3. Silvey, Anita, *Horn Book* (November–December 1985), 740.
4. Hall, Lynn, *The Giver* (New York: Scribner, 1985), 32; hereafter cited in text as *Giver*.
5. Rochman, Hazel, *Booklist*, 15 March 1985, 1050.
6. *Bulletin of the Center for Children's Books* (April 1985), 147.
7. Hall, Lynn, *Fair Maiden* (New York: Scribner, 1990), 1; hereafter cited in text as *Maiden*.
8. Belden, Elizabeth A., and Judith M. Beckman, "Finding New Harmony, Then and Now: Young Women's Rites of Passage," *English Journal* (September 1991), 85.
9. Zvirin, Stephanie, *Booklist*, 1 October 1990, 326.
10. Moore, Ann W., *School Library Journal* (November 1990), 138.
11. Hall, Lynn, *Flying Changes* (New York, Harcourt Brace Jovanovich, 1991), 27; hereafter cited in text as *Changes*.

12. Rochman, Hazel, *Booklist*, 15 June 1991, 1951.
13. Strickland, Charlene, *School Library Journal* (July 1991), 88.

Chapter 7

1. Hall, Lynn, *The Siege of Silent Henry* (Chicago: Follett, 1972), 93; hereafter cited in text as *Siege*.
2. *Kirkus*, 1 December 1972, 1358.
3. *Booklist*, 15 January 1973, 493.
4. Schrecengost, Diane, *Library Journal*, 15 May 1973, 1688.
5. Hall, Lynn, *Flowers of Anger* (Chicago: Follett, 1976), 8; hereafer cited in text as *Flowers*.
6. *Publishers Weekly*, 6 December 1969, 63.
7. Wilms, Denise M., *Booklist*, 15 January 1977, 718.
8. Hall, Lynn, *Just One Friend* (New York: Scribner, 1985), 1; hereafter cited in text as *Friend*.
9. Campbell, Patty, "The Young Adult Perplex," *Wilson Library Bulletin* (February 1986), 47.
10. Burns, Mary M., *Horn Book* (March–April 1986), 207.
11. Stark, Li, *School Library Journal* (December 1985), 88.
12. Hall, Lynn, *Where Have All the Tigers Gone?* (New York: Scribner, 1989), 10; hereafter cited in text as *Tigers*.
13. Porter, Judie, *School Library Journal* (May 1989), 126.
14. *Publishers Weekly*, 14 April 1989, 71.
15. Bodart, Joni, *Wilson Library Journal* (November 1989), 16.
16. Sheriff, Judith A., *Voice of Youth Advocates* (August 1989), 158.

Chapter 8

1. Nilsen, Alleen Pace, and Kenneth Donelson. *Literature for Today's Young Adults*, rev. ed. (Glenview: Scott, Foresman, 1985), 105–6; hereafter cited in text as Nilsen and Donelson.
2. Blume, Judy, *New York Times Book Review*, 28 May 1972, 8.

3. Hall, Lynn, *Sticks and Stones* (Chicago: Follett, 1972), 28–29; hereafter cited in text as *Sticks*.
4. *Publishers Weekly*, 14 Feburary 1972, 69.
5. Gerhardt, Lillian N., *School Library Journal* (November 1972), 75.
6. The original manuscript and drafts of the alternative endings cited are held in the Kerlan Collection, M.F. 393.
7. *Booklist*, 1 July 1972, 939.
8. The excerpts quoted are from letters contained in the Kerlan Collection, M.F. 393.

Chapter 9

1. Sutherland, Zena, *Children and Books*, 7th ed. (Glenview: Scott, Foresman, 1986), 374–75.
2. Burns, Connie Tyrrell, *School Library Journal* (January 1991), 92; and Susan Jelcich, *Voice of Youth Advocates* (December 1990), 282.
3. Sherman, Louise L., *School Library Journal* (December 1987), 85.
4. Sleeper, Kim, *Voice of Youth Advocates* (October 1987), 200–01.
5. Marcus, Susan F., *School Library Journal* (September 1988), 198.
6. Culberson, Delia A., *Voice of Youth Advocates* (December 1988), 238.
7. Hedge, Mary, *Voice of Youth Advocates* (April 1989), 28.
8. Greenfield, Judy, *School Library Journal* (January 1989), 94.
9. Hall, Lynn. *Murder in a Pig's Eye* (San Diego: Harcourt, Brace, Jovanovich, 1992), 16; hereafter cited in text as *Pig's Eye*.
10. Anderson, Beth E., *Voice of Youth Advocates* (October 1990), 218.
11. Fong, Doris A., *School Library Journal* (May 1990), 122.
12. Zvirin, Stephanie, *Booklist*, 15 March 1990, 1429.

Bibliography

PRIMARY WORKS

Young Adult Novels

Denison's Daughter. New York: Scribner, 1983
Fair Maiden. New York: Scribner, 1990
Flowers of Anger. Chicago: Follett, 1976
Flyaway. New York: Scribner, 1987
Flying Changes. San Diego: Harcourt Brace Jovanovich, 1991; HBJ, 1993
The Giver. New York: Scribner, 1985; Collier, 1987
Half the Battle. New York: Scribner, 1982
Halsey's Pride. New York: Scribner, 1990
If Winter Comes. New York: Scribner, 1986
Just One Friend. New York: Scribner, 1985; Collier, 1988
A Killing Freeze. New York: Morrow, 1988; Avon, 1990
The Leaving. New York: Scribner, 1980; Collier, 1988
Letting Go. New York: Scribner, 1987
Murder at the Spaniel Show. New York: Scribner, 1988
Murder in a Pig's Eye. San Diego: Harcourt Brace Jovanovich, 1990; HBJ, 1992
Ride a Dark Horse. New York: Morrow, 1987; Avon, 1988
The Siege of Silent Henry. Chicago: Follett, 1972
The Solitary. New York: Scribner, 1986; Collier, 1989
The Soul of the Silver Dog. San Diego: Harcourt Brace Jovanovich, 1992
Sticks and Stones. Chicago: Follett, 1972; Dell, 1979
Tin Can Tucker. New York: Scribner, 1982
Too Near the Sun. Chicago: Follett, 1970; Dell, 1972
Uphill All the Way. New York: Scribner, 1984
Where Have All the Tigers Gone? New York: Scribner, 1989
Windsong. New York: Scribner, 1992

Fiction for Younger Readers

Barry, the Bravest St. Bernard. Easton, Md.: Garrard, 1973; Random House, 1992

Between Friends. New York: Scribner, 1985

Bob, Watchdog of the River. Easton, Md.: Garrard, 1974

The Boy in the Off-White Hat. New York: Scribner, 1984

Captain: Canada's Flying Pony. Easton, Md.: Garrard, 1976

Dagmar Schultz and the Angel Edna. New York: Scribner, 1989; Aladdin, 1992

Dagmar Schultz and the Green-Eyed Monster. New York: Scribner, 1991

Dagmar Schultz and the Powers of Darkness. New York: Scribner, 1989; Aladdin, 1992

Danger Dog. New York: Scribner, 1986

Danza! New York: Scribner, 1981

The Disappearing Grandad. Chicago: Follett, 1980

Dog of Bondi Castle. Chicago: Follett, 1979

Dragon's Delight. Chicago: Follett, 1980

Dragon Defiant. Chicago: Follett, 1977

The Famous Battle of Bravery Creek. Easton, Md.: Garrard, 1972

Flash, Dog of Old Egypt. Easton, Md.: Garrard, 1973; Random House, 1992

Gently Touch the Milkweed. Chicago: Follett, 1970

The Ghost of the Great River Inn. Chicago: Follett, 1980

The Haunting of the Green Bird. Chicago: Follett, 1980

Here Comes Zelda Claus and Other Holiday Disasters. San Diego: Harcourt Brace Jovanovich, 1989

A Horse Called Dragon. Chicago: Follett, 1971

The Horse Trader. New York: Scribner, 1980

In Trouble Again, Zelda Hammersmith. San Diego: Harcourt Brace Jovanovich, 1987; Avon, 1989

Megan's Mare. New York: Scribner, 1983

Mrs. Portree's Pony. New York: Scribner, 1986

The Mystery of the Caramel Cat. Easton, Md.: Garrard, 1981

The Mystery of the Lost and Found Hound. Easton, Md.: Garrard, 1979

The Mysterious Moortown Bridge. Chicago: Follett, 1980

The Mystery of Plum Park Pony. Easton, Md.: Garrard, 1980; reissued as *The Mystery of the Phantom Pony,* Random House, 1993

The Mystery of Pony Hollow. Easton, Md.: Garrard, 1978; Random House, 1992

The Mystery of Pony Hollow Panda. Easton, Md.: Garrard, 1983

The Mystery of the Schoolhouse Dog. Easton, Md.: Garrard, 1979

The Mystery of the Stubborn Old Man. Easton, Md.: Garrard, 1980

New Day for Dragon. Chicago: Follett, 1975

Nobody's Dog. New York: Scholastic, 1984

Owney, the Traveling Dog. Easton, Md.: Garrard, 1977
Ride a Wild Dream. Chicago: Follett, 1969
Riff, Remember. Chicago: Follett, 1973
The Secret Life of Dagmar Schultz. New York: Scribner, 1988; Aladdin, 1991
The Secret of Stonehouse. Chicago: Follett, 1968
Shadows. Chicago: Follett, 1977; Knopf, 1992
The Shy Ones. Chicago: Follett, 1967
The Something-Special Horse. New York: Scribner, 1985
The Stray. Chicago: Follett, 1974
To Catch a Tartar. Chicago: Follett, 1973
The Tormentors. San Diego: Harcourt Brace Jovanovich, 1990
Troublemaker. Chicago: Follett, 1975
The Whispered Horse. Chicago: Follett, 1979
Zelda Strikes Again. San Diego: Harcourt Brace Jovanovich, 1988

Nonfiction

Careers for Dog Lovers. Chicago: Follett, 1978
Kids and Dog Shows. Chicago: Follett, 1975
Lynn Hall's Dog Stories. Chicago: Follett, 1972

SECONDARY WORKS

Biographical and Critical Studies

Brown, Joanne. "An Adolescent's Best Friend: The Role of Animals in Lynn Hall's Fiction." *ALAN Review* 21 (Spring 1994): 27–31
"Lynn Hall." In Commire, Anne, ed., *Something About the Author*, vol. 47, 97–104. Detroit: Gale Research, 1987
"Lynn Hall." In Holtze, Sally Holmes, ed., *Fifth Book of Junior Authors and Illustrators*, 145–47. New York: Wilson, 1983
"Lynn Hall." In Kirkpatrick, D. L., ed., *Twentieth–Century Children's Writers*, 2d ed., 351–53. New York: St. Martin's, 1983
"Lynn Hall." In Sarkissian, Adele, ed., *Something About the Author Autobiography Series*, vol. 4, 181–196. Detroit: Gale Research, 1987
Wilson, Ann K. "Lynn Hall: Solitary and Secure." *Signal* (Fall 1992):11–14

Book Reviews

Denison's Daughter
Hand, Dorcas, *Horn Book* (October 1983), 582
Sass, Rivkah, *Voice of Youth Advocates* (*VOYA*; April 1984), 30
Wilms, Denise M. *Booklist*, 15 September 1983, 171

Wood, Catherine, *School Library Journal* (November 1983), 92

Fair Maiden

Belden, Elizabeth, and Judith M. Beckman, "Finding New Harmony, Then and Now: Young Women's Rites of Passage," *English Journal* (September 1991), 85

Moore, Ann W., *School Library Journal* (November 1990), 138

Zvirin, Stephanie. *Booklist*, 1 October 1990, 326

Flowers of Anger

Publishers Weekly, 6 December 1976, 63

Wilms, Denise M., *Booklist*, 15 January 1977, 718

Flyaway

Ojibway, Mary, *VOYA* (December 1987), 235

Publishers Weekly, 25 September 1987, 112.

Zvirin, Stephanie, *Booklist*, 15 September 1987, 134

Flying Changes

Publishers Weekly, 31 May 1991, 77

Rochman, Hazel, *Booklist*, 15 June 1991, 1951

Strickland, Charlene, *School Library Journal* (July 1991), 88

The Giver

Bulletin of the Center for Children's Books (April 1985), 147.

MacDonald, Eleanor K., *School Library Journal* (August 1985), 75

Rochman, Hazel, *Booklist*, 1 June 1986, 1050

Silvey, Anita, *Horn Book* (November/December 1985), 740

Half the Battle

Chelton, Mary K., *VOYA* (August 1982), 31

Harris, Karen, *School Library Journal* (August 1982), 126

Zvirin, Stephanie, *Booklist*, 1 May 1982, 1153

Halsey's Pride

Mediatore, Kaite, *Wilson Library Bulletin* (January 1991), 8

Meisner, Sylvia V., *School Library Journal* (April 1990), 140

Pickworth, Hanna, *ALAN Review* (Fall 1991)

If Winter Comes

Connor, Anne, *School Library Journal* (September 1986), 133

Peasley, Rosie, *VOYA* (August/October 1986), 144

Publishers Weekly, 27 June 1986, 95

Rochman, Hazel, *Booklist*, 1 June 1986, 1454

Just One Friend

Burns, Mary M., *Horn Book* (March/April 1986), 207.

Campbell, Patty, *Wilson Library Bulletin* (February 1986), 47

Shelley, Margaret B., *English Journal* (November 1989), 80

Stark, Li, *School Library Journal* (December 1985), 88

A Killing Freeze
Culberson, Delia A., *VOYA* (December 1988), 238
Marcus, Susan F., *School Library Journal* (September 1988), 198
Zvirin, Stephanie, *Booklist* (August 1988), 1914

The Leaving
Bulletin of the Center for Children's Books (April 1981), 151
English Journal (September 1981), 77
Estes, Sally, *Booklist*, 1 October 1980, 206
Johnson, Becky, *VOYA* (February 1981), 30
Sprague, Sue, *School Library Journal* (December 1980), 63

Letting Go
Dean, Beth Wheeler, *VOYA* (June 1987), 78
Wilms, Denise M., *Booklist*, 15 April 1987, 1289

Murder at the Spaniel Show
Greenfield, Judy, *School Library Journal* (January 1989), 92
Hedge, Mary, *VOYA* (April 1989), 28
Rochman, Hazel, *Booklist*, 1 December 1988, 640

Murder in a Pig's Eye
Anderson, Beth E., *VOYA* (October 1990), 218
Fong, Doris A., *School Library Journal* (May 1990), 122
Zvirin, Stephanie, *Booklist*, 15 March 1990, 1429

Ride a Dark Horse
Rochman, Hazel, *Booklist*, 15 September 1987, 134
Sherman, Louise L., *School Library Journal* (December 1987), 85
Sleeper, Kim, *VOYA* (October 1987), 200–01

The Siege of Silent Henry
Booklist, 15 January 1973, 493
Kirkus, 1 December 1972, 1358
Schrecengost, Diane, *Library Journal*, 15 May 1973, 1688

The Solitary
Beatty, Cynthia L., *VOYA* (February 1987), 285
Butler, Judy M. *School Library Journal* (January 1987), 82
Hearne, Betsy, *Bulletin of the Center for Children's Books* (December 1986), 68
Zvirin, Stephanie. *Booklist,* 15 November 1986, 502

The Soul of the Silver Dog
McCarthy, Carrol, *School Library Journal* (June 1992), 136
Rochman, Hazel, *Booklist*, 15 April 1992, 1522

Sticks and Stones
Blume, Judy, *New York Times Book Review,* 28 May 1972, 8
Booklist, 1 July 1972, 939

Bulletin of the Center for Children's Books (October 1972), 25
Gerhardt, Lillian N., *School Library Journal* (November 1972), 75
Publishers Weekly, 14 Febuary 1972, 69

Tin Can Tucker
Burns, Mary M., *Horn Book* (October 1982), 519
Zvirin, Stephanie. *Booklist*, 1 September 1982, 36

Too Near the Sun
Bulletin of the Center for Children's Books (October 1970), 11
Dorsey, Margaret A., *Library Journal,* 15 May 1970, 1953
English Journal (September 1972), 935
Kirkus Reviews, 15 May 1970, 552

Uphill All the Way
Copan, Mary Lynn, *School Library Journal* (May 1984), 89
Nelms, Beth, Ben Nelms, and Linda Horton, *English Journal* (January 1985), 93–94
Zvirin, Stephanie, *Booklist*, 1 April 1984, 1110

Where Have All the Tigers Gone?
Bodart, Joni, *Wilson Library Journal* (November 1989), 16
Porter, Judie, *School Library Journal* (May 1989), 126
Publishers Weekly, 14 April 1989, 71
Rochman, Hazel, *Booklist*, 15 April 1989, 1455
Sheriff, Judith A., *VOYA* (August 1989), 158

Windsong
Burner, Joyce Adams, *School Library Journal* (November 1992), 122
Stapleton, Margaret M., *VOYA* (February 1993), 339
Zvirin, Stephanie, *Booklist*, 1 November 1992, 509

Index

The Author

Susan Stan has served as editor of *The Five Owls,* a publication about children's literature, since its inception in 1986. She is completing a Ph.D. in literacy education at the University of Minnesota.

The Editor

Patricia J. Campbell is an author and critic specializing in books for young adults. She has taught adolescent literature at UCLA and is the former Assistant Coordinator of Young Adult Services for Los Angeles Public Library. Her literary criticism has been published in the *New York Times Book Review* and many other journals. From 1978 to 1988 her column "The YA Perplex," a monthly review of young adult books, appeared in the *Wilson Library Bulletin*. She now writes a review column about the independent press for that magazine and a column about controversial issues in adolescent literature for *Horn Book* magazine. Campbell is the author of five books, among them *Presenting Robert Cormier,* the first volume in Twayne's Young Adult Authors Series. In 1989 she was the recipient of the American Library Association Grolier Award for distinguished achievement with young people and books. A native of Los Angeles, Campbell now lives on an avocado ranch near San Diego, where she and her husband, David Shore, write and publish books about overseas motor-home travel.